T0062448

Order this book online at www.trafford.com
or email orders@trafford.com

Most Trafford titles are also available at major online book retailers.

Printed in Victoria, BC, Canada.

ISBN: 978-1-4269-1506-2 (sc)
ISBN: 978-1-4269-1507-9 (hc)

Library of Congress Control Number: 2009913677

*Our mission is to efficiently provide the world's finest, most comprehensive
book publishing service, enabling every author to experience success.
To find out how to publish your book, your way, and have it available
worldwide, visit us online at www.trafford.com*

Trafford rev. 2/11/2010

 www.trafford.com

North America & international
toll-free: 1 888 232 4444 (USA & Canada)
phone: 250 383 6864 ♦ fax: 812 355 4082

Acknowledgement:

In writing this book, I am indebted to many people and will like to acknowledge as many as possible.

I am a product of many meetings. I have many teachers, most notable being Bishop T.D Jakes, Pastor Kenneth Hagin Snr. and Joel Osteen, but I have only one father. He is my confidant, coach, mentor and pastor – Rev Chris Oyakhilome. His influence over my life and this book is unquantifiable. He has also given me time-tested leaders that have continued to water my garden of faith – Pastors Lanre Alabi, Deola Okeowo, Ifeoma Chiemeka, Oshoke Imoagene, and Dolapo Layode.

I am also very grateful to my fellow servants in God's vineyard at the breakfast fellowship in my place of work – Sina Ayegbusi, Tunde Dawodu, Chima Nwankwo, Azu Okonkwo, and Onome Komolafe.

My friends helped me to reduce the errors in this book and I want to appreciate their invaluable contributions – Eno Ebito, Opeoluwa Bamiro, Patrick Kasie Nwachukwu, Morayo Osanyinjobi and Abimbola Dosunmu. Kehinde Olaposii, Samuel Omotayo, and Gabriel Olonisakin did all the technical work – graphics, typesetting and interior design.

I also want to thank my lovely wife, Sandra Aluba, and adorable Sons, David Ifeanyichukwu, and Daniel Ikechukwu for their understanding and sacrifice while I worked on the book.

Forward

'Watch Out World, I'm coming out' is a captivating book. It reveals the insight into God's word that the author, Michael Ogbaa has received, and reflects the message of the divine life as revealed by the Man of God, Pastor Chris. This book shows what it is to live the life of glory and virtue – a life available to all who have received Jesus Christ as Lord. I recommend the book as a must read to anyone who seeks answers to hitherto unresolved questions.

Pastor Oshoke Imoagene

International President

The Haven

Believers Love World (Christ Embassy Church)

Dedication

This book is dedicated to all the preachers of the glorious gospel of Jesus Christ and everybody that contributes in ensuring that the word of God covers the world as the waters cover the sea.

Prologue

I am an incurable optimist. I got 'infected' the day I discovered who I am in Christ. By the time you read half of this book, you will understand what happened to me. You will realise that you are the object of God's love, the personality of His deepest affection, the apple of His eyes and His treasure of inestimable value!

The Chinese Bamboo

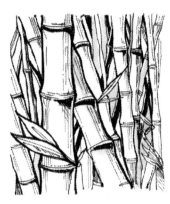

...your testimony will be liken to that of the bamboo tree - NINETY FEET IN SIX WEEKS!

I'm always encouraged each time I remember the story of the Chinese bamboo Tree.

You take a little seed, plant it, water it, and fertilize it for a whole year, and nothing happens. The second year you water it and fertilize it, and nothing happens. The third year you water it and fertilize it, and nothing happens. How discouraging this becomes!

You continue to water and fertilize the seed through the fourth and fifth year and then ... Take note, sometime during the fifth year, the Chinese bamboo tree sprouts and grows NINETY FEET IN SIX WEEKS!

Jesus Christ after He was born watered His life for thirty long years and it seemed as if nothing happened! However, after the Holy Ghost had come upon Him, He started turning dish-water to wine, healing the sick and raising the dead. Spoke to the wind and the wave, the tree and miracles happened!

I don't know where you are in your life, I don't know what situation and circumstances you may be passing through, but one thing I do know is that if you keep watering your bamboo tree of faith, regardless of how long it takes, your reward, your result, indeed your testimony will be liken to that of the bamboo tree - NINETY FEET IN SIX WEEKS!

Galatians 6:9 - And let us not be weary in well doing: for in due season we shall reap, if we faint not.

The Violinist

There was a boy that dreamt of becoming the world's best violinist. To achieve his life desire, he sold all his belongings and traveled to a faraway land where the renowned and best violinist of all time lived.

The apartment he was directed to was in a solitary place, old, and unkempt. There was no evidence of life whatsoever. The young man was disappointed and turned to leave. Then he heard someone coughing from within.

The renowned violinist was very old and dying. He refused to teach the young boy, who also refused to leave. The boy played the old man's violin at midnights, and this he did for 3 nights till the old man could not bear it any more. He came out on the fourth night and began to coach the boy.

Fast-forward. It was the biggest violin competition in the world. The young man was amongst the hundreds of contestants. The event lasted for days. On the day he played, everyone was in tears. First, the boy was so young, but no violin master of all times could have played better. Second, the boy was focused on empty space and never looked elsewhere till he finished. Third, only tears came down his focused eyes and he was not distracted by it.

He was crowned the champion!

Only the boy knew the reason for his success. Apart from learning from the best violinist the world ever knew, the old man had come in person that day and had directed him from the gallery even when it wasn't obvious to anyone around. The old man died few days later.

Hebrews 12:2 - Looking unto Jesus the author and finisher of our faith; who for the joy that was set before him endured the cross, despising the shame, and is set down at the right hand of the throne of God.

> **...the boy was focused on empty space and never looked elsewhere until he finished.**

The Camera

...at some point loved the pictures they saw .. nothing stopped them from bringing them to reality

I worked in a photo lab for six months before my current place of employment. Though I was the Manager of the head office of the company, I trained myself to be one of the best photo printers in the company.

It was during this period that I learnt how cameras work. They operate with the principle of reflection. The image you focus the camera on is what is reflected on the film stored within the camera. This is exactly what is developed in a dark environment and printed as pictures (or photos). Isn't life a big camera? Think about it, all the products, all the services, and all the companies around you – COMPAQ computers, First Bank, Zenith Bank, NIKE, Microsoft, CNN, MTN, SONY, Redeemed Christian Church Of God, Christ Embassy Church, Mercedes Benz, ETC are the printed images and visions of men and women like you and I! The only difference is that the people who had these visions within them at some point loved the pictures they saw in their minds so much that nothing stopped them from bringing them to reality! What picture do you see in your mind? Can you let the world see it?

The reflection principle is not any different from the mirror principle found in the Bible...

2 Corinthians 3:18 - But we all, with open face beholding as in a glass the glory of the Lord, are changed into the same image from glory to glory, even as by the Spirit of the Lord.

Sound Barrier

God is awesome. Anytime I have the opportunity of flying, I'm humbled by the awesomeness of God. As any frequent flyer will tell you, the plane passes through the most turbulent phase when it is breaking through the sound barrier to enter into the smoothest part of the flight!

How come it is darkest just before the break of dawn? Why did the devil tempt Jesus immediately He finished fasting in the wilderness and was at His greatest spiritual high? The answer is simple. Our patience and our faith are always keenly tested just before our victories and miracles!

Are you passing through the most turbulent period of your life? Are the circumstances around you becoming unbearable? Then, you might as well start popping champagnes and praising God because your miracle is a step away!

Count it all joy when you fall into various trials, knowing that the testing of your faith produces faith – James 1:2-3.

Remember that weeping may endure for a night, but joy comes in the morning!

The Law Of Gravity

Just want us to meditate on one of the oldest and yet easiest-to- prove laws of nature – the law of gravity - anything that goes up must come down! You can drop anything you have in your hand right now, and most assuredly, it must obey the law of gravity!

But as universal and powerful as the law of gravity is, man, yes, mere man has introduced higher laws and principles that have defied and invalidated the law of gravity! One of such laws is the law of aerodynamics – the law that makes an airplane to disobey the law of gravity; it's the law that takes man to the moon. How about a small balloon, even the ones people use at weddings, once you fill them with helium, they start disobeying the law of gravity.

...the law that makes an airplane to disobey the law of gravity

Now, read the laws of Jehovah (which supersedes every other law)!

John 16:33 ... but be of good cheer; I have overcome the world.

1 John 5:4 - For whatsoever is born of God overcometh the world: and this is the victory that overcometh the world, even our faith.

1 John 4:4 - Ye are of God, little children, and have overcome them: because greater is he that is in you, than he that is in the world.

Brothers and Sisters, these things are not difficult to understand or to believe, if ordinary inert gas makes a balloon to rise above the law of nature, what do you think the Spirit of God, mixed with faith in God will do in the life of a man?

Unlimited

The last time I checked, only one company in Nigeria had the title "unlimited" before its name – Mobil Unlimited.

Very instructive. What this means is that the shareholders of Mobil have so much trust and confidence in the company that they are saying that their liabilities (the extent to which debtors to the company can go in recovering their debts if the company is liquidated) is unlimited! Wow!

I would have been overwhelmed by such confidence, but after Titanic sank, after Enron collapsed, after Arthur Andersen went into oblivion overnight, I now know better than to trust the words of men.

There is only One Person whose powers are unlimited, whose love is beyond comprehension, whose grace is sufficient, whose words can be trusted without questions – His Name is Jesus!

Psalms 118:8 - It is better to trust in the LORD than to put confidence in man.

Proverbs 3:5 - Trust in the LORD with all thine heart; and lean not unto thine own understanding.

Opportunity Cost

I spent four years in the university studying Economics. One of the basic topics every economist must learn to obtain a BSc certificate in Economics is the principle of "opportunity cost".

Opportunity Cost is defined as the forgone alternative. Due to limited resources, the real cost of our choices are the things we need to forgo to have the ones we choose. If a man has $4 million which could either build him a bungalow or buy him a BMW car, the real cost (opportunity cost) of buying the car is the house he has to forgo and vice versa.

In the same vein, if you want to know how valuable you are to God, then look at Jesus Christ hanging at the cross of Calvary! God wants me to inform you today that the real cost (opportunity cost) of allowing His begotten Son to die (the only time They were separated) was because of you!

John 3:16 - For God so loved the world, that he gave his only begotten Son, that whosoever believeth in him should not perish, but have everlasting life.

Laying Aside Every Weight

I have often wondered why athletes wear as little dress as possible. Then I read the following verse of the bible and understood why...

Hebrews 12:1 - Wherefore seeing we also are compassed about with so great a cloud of witnesses, let us lay aside every weight, and the sin which doth so easily beset us, and let us run with patience the race that is set before us.

Brethren, when you are in a serious race, every little weight defeats your aim by weighing you down. The weight that might deny you heaven might be your friends, your family, your job, your hobbies, and your education. Anything whatever! Please, lay them aside, nothing can be better than spending eternity with Jesus!

The Last Order

One of the main reasons why I like the military is because of their discipline – the ability and training of military men to obey orders.

There are no excuses; they only obey the last order from their highest-ranking officers.

The Bible tells us that we are soldiers and as soldiers, we have a Commander In Chief Whose last order we (as faithful soldiers) must obey!

Our Commander In Chief is Jesus Christ and this is His last order to us...

"Go ye therefore, and teach all nations, baptizing them in the name of the Father, and of the Son, and of the Holy Ghost" - Matthew 28:19.

Mighty Soldiers, let's obey the last order!

2 Timothy 2:4 - No man that warreth entangleth himself with the affairs of this life; that he may please him who hath chosen him to be a soldier.

Intel Inside

Cloned computers are very common these days as many people don't really see any difference between cloned and branded computers. But let the truth be told, when heavy duty assignments are required, when tons of commands are given to the computer within a short period of time, the differences would become obvious.

The most reliable computers, I have come to observe are the ones with "Intel inside". These are computers with Intel microprocessors which are the most reliable in the whole world!

Is it not the same in the spiritual world? At a bus-stop, a man dramatically falls to the ground and suffers from epileptic seizure, all the "cloned" people run away, but the "Intel inside" person walks up to him and heals him through the Holy Ghost.

When all the "cloned" staff are running helter skelter calling for first aids, doctors, ambulances etc because a colleague has fainted, "The Holy Spirit inside" colleague will rise up to the occasion lay Holy Hands and revive the staff!

In your neighborhood, it is 1 am and everybody (cloned people) is crying and wailing, calling the hospitals and the mortuary because a six-year old child has just died. You, with "The Holy Spirit inside" will come out, having been endued with power from on high and revive the dead child!

You would not need the power of the Holy Spirit in heaven; you have been empowered to influence your world!

Acts 1:8 - But ye shall receive power, after that the Holy Ghost is come upon you: and ye shall be witnesses unto me both in Jerusalem, and in all Judaea, and in Samaria, and unto the uttermost part of the earth.

1 John 4:4 - Ye are of God, little children, and have overcome them: because greater is he that is in you, than he that is in the world.

> **...When all the "cloned" staff are running helter skater calling for first aids, ... because your colleague has fainted,**

Turn To the Wall

Isaiah 38:2 - Then Hezekiah turned his face toward the wall, and prayed unto the LORD.

Certain situations require certain actions. King Hezekiah was told by God (through a prophet of God) that he should prepare to die! The Bible says that he turned away from the whole world, from every other thing in life, faced the wall and settled the matter with God! His life was prolonged!

Elijah understood this principle of separation when he put his face between his knees (away from everything else in the world) and prayed for rain. Rain indeed came!

...faced the wall and settled the matter with God!

Now the biggest one. The Bible records that Jesus Christ prayed alone when he had serious issues to settle. He separated Himself from everybody else!

I don't know what serious matter you want to settle, maybe it's time you turned to the wall!

1 Kings 18:42 - So Ahab went up to eat and to drink. And Elijah went up to the top of Carmel; and he cast himself down upon the earth, and put his face between his knees.

Expert Opinion

The world is full of experts in all walks of life. Since the beginning of time, we have never had these experts in short supply.

Isaac sowed in a land in which experts believed could not produce anything, but Isaac sowed in that land, and received in the same year a hundredfold: and the LORD blessed him - Genesis 26:12.

Field Marshals, war Generals and experts concluded that it was impossible for the Israelites to take their enemy territories, but "inexperienced" Joshua and Caleb believed God rather than the experts. They were the only ones God spared when His Word came to pass.

Elisha prophesied, "Tomorrow about this time shall a measure of fine flour be sold for a shekel, and two measures of barley for a shekel, in the gate of Samaria". The Finance Minister of Israel, the country's best financial expert explained to the King that it was financially, fiscally, economically (considering all the macro and micro economic indexes), impossible for Elisha's prophesy to be true. He died as an expert while the Word of God came to pass.

Simon Peter was a disciple of Jesus Christ. He was not just older than Jesus; he was also an expert in fishing. He knew that it was impossible to catch fish at a certain time of the night and at certain places… "we have toiled all the night, and have taken nothing: nevertheless at thy word I will let down the net". Against his expert opinion, he had the most amazing experience of his life as a fisherman that day by subduing his expert opinion to God's Opinion.

Then the biggest one! It is medically, scientifically and biologically impossible for conception to take place without the fusion of an egg from a woman and a sperm from a man. Mary knew this; Joseph knew this and when God (with whom there are no limitations and barriers) wanted to alter the course of nature, He knew that "experts" would deceive Joseph, so He sent an angel to him to prepare him! Then the biggest miracle of all times took place – a virgin had God's baby! God's Word was the "sperm".

Brothers and Sisters, I don't know what financial, psychological, medical, economic, social, political and other experts might have told you regarding your situations and circumstances in life, but this very thing I know and believe: Jehovah is God's name which means "causes to become". With God, all things are possible! Even if the solution to your problem has never been heard of before, Jehovah will create it!

Experiment 101

I do not know how many of us studied Chemistry in secondary schools back in the day, but let's try our hands on something very simple today when we get home. Pour some water in a white or glass container. Add a small drop of oil (any type of oil will do – Vaseline, palm oil, vegetable oil, engine oil, any type you can easily get). Observe what will happen. The oil will certainly float on top of the water!

It does not matter where, when, who or how the experiment is done, the result is assured. The oil represents you and I, the water typify circumstances, challenges and cares of this world while the container symbolizes the world!

Come what may, we would forever be on top!

John 16:33 - These things I have spoken unto you, that in me ye might have peace. In the world ye shall have tribulation: but be of good cheer; I have overcome the world.

Romans 8:37 - Nay, in all these things we are more than conquerors through him that loved us.

Keep floating!

Henry Ford

At the turn of the 20th century, a man was testing his greatest possession of that time – an automobile. As he drove his car down the streets of California, it came to a halt for reasons he had no clue about. The car owner was frustrated as he sat there helpless and hapless for hours.

Incidentally, a similar car pulled over with its owner, without waiting to be asked, fixed the car in record time. Overjoyed at such a magical (miraculous) help, the guy whose car was fixed offered some money to his helper.

"Please don't worry about giving me money, if anything, I should be the one offering you money for your discomfort. My name is Henry Ford, I built the car, and it was not meant to function the way it did".

Henry Ford was concerned about his reputation as a car maker.

Do you know that we are God's own handiwork?

Ephesians 2:10 – For we are His workmanship, created in Christ Jesus for good works, which God prepared beforehand that we should work in them.

Knock Knock

Fear knocked at the door; Faith answered
but there was nobody at the door!

*Mark 4:40 - And he said unto them, Why are ye
so fearful? how is it that ye have no faith?*

Speed of Light

I did a little research which I want to share with us. The Japanese Shinkansen line is currently the fastest train in the world with a top speed of 186 miles per hour; the Shinkansen Bullet Train averages 162 miles an hour between Hiroshima and Kokura stations. The speed of sound at sea level is 340.29m/s. The SR-71 is the fastest airplane made by man. It flies at 33 miles per minute or 3,000 feet per second. It flies faster than a 30-06 bullet. Its speed is three times the speed of sound. It out-flies the sun. You can have breakfast in New York; fly to Los Angeles (in a Blackbird), have another breakfast (time wise) before you leave New York.

Fast as the speed of the sound and the fastest airplane are, the speed of light is 299,792,458m/s. Wow! There is nothing under heaven that can be faster than the speed of light. Or so I thought till I read my Bible!

The only thing faster than the speed of light is "the speed of prayer!"

Acts 12:12 – 16 - And when he had considered the thing, he came to the house of Mary the mother of John, whose surname was Mark; where many were gathered together praying. And as Peter knocked at the door of the gate, a damsel came to hearken, named Rhoda. And when she knew Peter's voice, she opened not the gate for gladness, but ran in, and told how Peter stood before the gate. And they said unto her, Thou art mad. But she constantly affirmed that it was even so. Then said they, It is his angel. But Peter continued knocking: and when they had opened the door, and saw him, they were astonished.

Time will fail me to talk about the speed of the prayers of Abraham, Moses, Joshua, Esther and Mordecai, David, Elijah, Elisha, Jesus Christ and The Apostles.

I dare you to try the speed of prayer if you are in doubt!

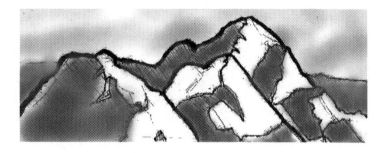

Levels

As you reign in life today as priests and kings unto God, I just want you to remember that the same flood that wiped away Noah's generation was what uplifted his boat!

Lot's wife turned into a pillar of salt when she looked at the burning Sodom and Gomorrah, but Abraham also looked at the same burning city from a mountain top and didn't suffer the same fate!

Brothers and Sisters, there are levels in God!

Genesis 19:26 – 28 - But his wife looked back from behind him, and she became a pillar of salt. And Abraham gat up early in the morning to the place where he stood before the LORD. And he looked toward Sodom and Gomorrah, and toward all the land of the plain, and beheld, and, lo, the smoke of the country went up as the smoke of a furnace.

Romans 8:1 - There is therefore now no condemnation to them which are in Christ Jesus, who walk not after the flesh, but after the Spirit.

1 Timothy 1:9 - Knowing this, that the law is not made for a righteous man, but for the lawless and disobedient, for the ungodly and for sinners, for unholy and profane, for murderers of fathers and murderers of mothers, for manslayers,

Overheard In an Orchard

Said the Robin to the Sparrow:

"I should really like to know
Why these anxious human beings
Rush about and worry so"

Said the Sparrow to the Robin:

"Friend, I think that it must be
That they have no
Heavenly Father
Such as cares for you and me"
-Elizabeth Cheney

Psalms 37:1 Fret not thyself...

*Philippians 4:6 - Be careful for nothing; but in everything
by prayer and supplication with thanksgiving let your
requests be made known unto God.*

*Matthew 10:31 - Fear ye not therefore, ye are of more value
than many sparrows.*

When Jesus Comes Late

Have you ever been in a situation where you felt that God delayed just a little bit in answering your prayers? Are you going through a difficult time where you wish that Jesus ought to do something really fast before things get out of hand? Then, you are exactly the person God wants to minister to today!

John 11:21 Then said Martha unto Jesus, Lord, if thou hadst been here (a little earlier), my brother had not died.

Who created time? Who is it that is not bound by time or circumstances? Who is it that can go back in time, is on top of the present and can catapult Himself into the future and change anything and everything? Yes, His Name is Jesus!

Brothers and Sisters, when Jesus comes late, you might as well gather trumpeters, roll out the drums and start popping champagnes because He is bringing resurrection and life to any dead situation, any dead circumstance, any dead business, any dead person, any dead vision in your life!

John 11:25 - Jesus said unto her, I am the resurrection, and the life: he (anything) that believeth in me, though he (the circumstance or situation) were dead, yet shall he (that thing you have given up on) live.

When Jesus shows up late, He only does so to build your faith and be rest assured, He will certainly restore the thing you were anxious about better than you can ever imagine!

John 11:14 Then said Jesus unto them plainly, Lazarus is dead. 15 And I am glad for your sakes that I was not there, to the intent ye may believe; nevertheless let us go unto him.

Ecclesiastes 3:11 - He hath made every thing beautiful in his time.

The Breasted One

God indeed is our Super Mama, the Strong and Breasted One!

Jehovah Rapha is the Strong and Breasted One. Pastor T.D Jakes once preached the Breastedness of God into my spirit. Any Mother will tell you that after child-birth, the breast naturally gets filled with milk. Any mother will also tell you that nothing in the world could be more frustrating than having the baby cry and wail for breast-milk which the mother is more willing to give it than it desires to have.

The mother loves the baby more than the baby loves itself. She knows that the baby's life depends on her breast-milk and naturally will be more than willing to feed her baby. But, more than all these, the mother's breast aches when she does not feed the child! Yes, she loves her baby and wants to satisfy it, but she loves herself also and wants to relieve herself of the ache caused by the overflowing food for her child!

Brethren, God is displeased when we wail and cry for His help when all He ever wants is for us to just shut up so that He can feed us!

God has an overflowing blessings and inheritance meant only for us since He can't use them! What do you think God wants to do with the cattle upon a thousand hills? (Psalms 50:10 - For every beast of the forest is mine, and the cattle upon a thousand hills). His streets are paved with gold, so all the gold in world are for His kids! If He could offer Jesus for our sakes, what is it that He could ever withhold from us?

God indeed is our Super Mama, the Strong and Breasted One!

Psalms 46:1 - God is our refuge and strength, a very present help in trouble.

If you have ever been to a shipyard, you will appreciate the role anchors play. An anchor is simply a mechanical device that prevents a vessel from moving. It is a central cohesive source of support and stability to anything tied to it.

The size of a vessel does not matter, the weight of a ship does not matter, and the nature of the boat does not count. Come rain or high waters, let the tempest and waves come, be it turbulence, be it storm, be it hail, if the anchor is strong, the vessel, the ship, the boat, the yacht, etc will be secured.

Brothers and Sisters, Jesus Christ is our Anchor. Weapons would certainly be formed against us, enemies would certainly gather against us, we shall certainly be troubled on every side, we might be perplexed at times, we shall certainly be persecuted, and we shall be cast down, but since our Anchor is Jesus, we shall with certainty, without a shadow of doubt individually repeat what Paul said "But none of these things move me, neither count I my life dear unto myself, so that I might finish my course with joy, and the ministry, which I have received of the Lord Jesus, to testify the gospel of the grace of God" – Acts 20:24.

Romans 8: 35-37 Who shall separate us from the love of Christ? Shall tribulation, or distress, or persecution, or famine, or nakedness, or peril, or sword? As it is written, For thy sake we are killed all the daylong; we are accounted as sheep for the slaughter. Nay, in all these things we are more than conquerors through him that loved us.
2 Corinthians 4:8 We are troubled on every side, yet not distressed; we are perplexed, but not in despair; [9] Persecuted, but not forsaken; cast down, but not destroyed.
Psalms 40:2 - He brought me up also out of an horrible pit, out of the miry clay, and set my feet upon a rock, and established my goings.

Callous Me

They say that I'm callous, insensitive, thick-skinned, uncaring, hardened and unperturbed about things. Maybe they're right, maybe they're not.

Here is the reason. Each time someone tells me any "bad news" thinking that I'll be shocked, dazed, worried, agitated, cast down, or dismayed my answer has always been the same. I'll ask the person if God is dead. If the answer is no, then, the situation cannot be as serious as anybody may think!

I know too much of the Bible to know that nothing is irreparable or impossible with God! He does resurrect dead things remember.

Since in Him all things consist (Colossians 1:17), since He calls me the apple of His eyes (Zechariah 2:8), since

He says that I am graven upon the palms of His hands (Isaiah 49:16), since He has said that He will never leave me nor forsake me (Hebrews 13:5), since He said that He will be with me always (Matthew 28:20), since He never sleeps nor slumbers because of me (Psalms 121:4), since I know the thoughts He has for me, thoughts of peace, and not of evil, to give me an expected end (Jeremiah 29:11), since all things work together for my good (Romans 8:28), since in everything I am more than a conqueror (Romans 8:37), since I know that greater is He that is in me, than he that is in the world (1 John 4:4), and so many other scriptures, you can understand why I cannot be moved by any circumstance or situation!

Maybe I'm not callous after all, what do you think?

Bull Riders

One of the most dangerous sports known to man is the Spanish bull-fighting. Bull-riders are the greatest risk-takers I know. If you have seen this sport on television like I have, you must have noticed that those bulls are never friendly at all, if anything, they look mad. They are known to have killed their riders in the past.

Nevertheless, the greatest bull-riders are the ones that stay the longest on top of raging bulls! The greatest oaks are the ones that withstand the greatest storms. The best sailors are the ones that train in the deadliest seas. Olympic Gold Medalists are those few that continue after everyone else gives up!

As Christians, our best qualities are revealed when we pass through our greatest trials in life! We should never be afraid to ride the bulls of life.

James 1:2-3 - My brethren, count it all joy when ye fall into divers temptations; Knowing this, that the trying of your faith worketh patience.

When Apostle Paul was warned not to go to Jerusalem to avoid being killed (like people beg their loved ones not to risk their lives as bull-riders), he made one of the greatest statements in the entire Bible!

Acts 20:24 - But none of these things move me, neither count I my life dear unto myself, so that I might finish my course with joy, and the ministry, which I have received of the Lord Jesus, to testify the gospel of the grace of God.

Brethren, Satan can use his deadliest weapons on us, but we know the end of the matter, don't we?

Seeing Through God's Lenses

Isaiah 55:9 - For as the heavens are higher than the earth, so are my ways higher than your ways, and my thoughts than your thoughts.

I'm greatly amazed when I meditate on some aspects of God.

Ishmael was an illegitimate son of Abraham whom Abraham persuaded God to accept and bless. This is what God said about Ishmael... "And as for Ishmael, I have heard thee: Behold, I have blessed him, and will make him fruitful, and will multiply him exceedingly; twelve princes shall he beget, and I will make him a great nation." - Genesis 17:20.

Years later, when God's plans for Abraham started manifesting and Abraham expressed the greatest act of faith by offering Isaac to God; this is what God said... "And he said, Lay not thine hand upon the lad, neither do thou any thing unto him: for now I know that thou fearest God, seeing thou hast not withheld thy son, thine only son from me" - Genesis 22:12.

Question: How come God called Isaac Abraham's ONLY son?
Read your Bible, God never called Moses a murderer in spite of overwhelming evidence to that fact. Rahab's name is very conspicuous in the hall of faith in Hebrews 11, yet, you and I know that she was not just a prostitute, but also a liar!

Brethren, my point is this, while we should care about what people say about us, our ultimate judge, our ultimate standard, the ultimate opinion that should matter to us above all else, should be God's!

"Yet"

As children of prophesy, we know how important spoken Words are. Where we are today (everything considered) is as a result of what we said in time past! Where we shall be tomorrow is going to be crafted (created, framed, actualized) by what we are saying today!

I just want to encourage us to start using a simple but great word that irritates the devil so much while at the same time helps us to craft our blissful future. That word is simply "yet".

Instead of saying I do not have money, why not say "I do not have the money yet", I do not have the job yet, I do not have the car yet, we do not have our baby yet, we have not moved to our own house yet, I am not married yet, etc.

Whenever you use the word "yet', satan gets mad because you are warning him not to write you off yet, you are practically telling him that using your faith as your life-jacket, that though you have been pushed into the ocean of uncertainty, you can never be drowned! "Yet" makes the devil mad because it reminds him that though he has mercilessly knocked you down today, the fight is not yet over till you win! (The Referee is Jesus).

Psalms 30:5 - For his anger endureth but a moment; in his favour is life: weeping may endure for a night, but joy cometh in the morning.

There is a victor inside of you, there's a champion inside of you, there's a winner inside of you, there's a blessed man inside of you, there's an entrepreneur inside of you, there's a billionaire inside of you!

It's not over, YET!

Burn Your Boat!

Esther 4:16 ... and so will I go in unto the king, which is not according to the law: and if I perish, I perish.

The most heroic battles of the Second World War took place in Asia. Some contingents of American Army used what I'm sure they must have copied from the Bible:

Luke 9:62 - And Jesus said unto him, No man, having put his hand to the plough, and looking back, is fit for the kingdom of God.

When these military men entered an enemy territory, they burnt their boats! The implication was so obvious; either they win the battle or they perish! The rest is history.

Brothers and Sisters, our Christian faith, our evangelistic ministry, our gospel financing, indeed, our walk with God should also be a matter of "no retreat, no surrender". There should be no "fall-back" position. We should be totally sold out to God!

Most times in life, our past has been proven to be the greatest enemy of our future. But for Caleb and Joshua (who had a different Spirit), every other person that left Egypt died in the wilderness because of their nostalgia for the past:

Numbers 11:5-6 - We remember the fish, which we did eat in Egypt freely; the cucumbers, and the melons, and the leeks, and the onions, and the garlick. But now our soul is dried away: there is nothing at all, beside this manna, before our eyes.

Brethren, let's burn our boats; the Lord will surely fight our battles!

Someone Somewhere Is Restless Because of You!

Isaac didn't do anything that made God bless him abundantly; God blessed him simply because of Abraham! Aren't you Abraham's seed?

Genesis 26:24 - And the LORD appeared unto him the same night, and said, I am the God of Abraham thy father: fear not, for I am with thee, and will bless thee, and multiply thy seed for my servant Abraham's sake.

King David could not stand disable people. But Mephibosheth was Jonathan's son, yet lame in both legs. David didn't rest till the day he blessed this Jonathan's seed!

2 Samuel 9:7 - And David said unto him, Fear not: for I will surely shew thee kindness for Jonathan thy father's sake, and will restore thee all the land of Saul thy father; and thou shalt eat bread at my table continually.

When God remembered Mordecai, King Ahasuerus could not sleep till Mordecai was blessed in spite of the plans to kill him!

Esther 6:1 On that night could not the king sleep, and he commanded to bring the book of records of the chronicles ...3 And the king said, What honour and dignity hath been done to Mordecai for this?

Read your Bible, the woman whom Jesus healed just because she was Abraham's Seed neither prayed nor expected her healing! (Luke 13:12;16 - And when Jesus saw her, he called her to him, and said unto her, Woman, thou art loosed from thine infirmity. And ought not this woman, being a daughter of Abraham, whom Satan hath bound, lo, these eighteen years, be loosed from this bond?).

Dearest, somebody somewhere is restless because of your blessing! Aren't you a joint-heir with Jesus? Aren't you Abraham's seed? You are more than qualified for any blessing, no matter how great!

Conveyor

Every airport has a conveyor, an apparatus for moving passenger's belongings from the plane to the airport in a continuous fashion. This is accomplished with an endless (that is, looped) procession of hooks, buckets, wide rubber belt, etc.

Do you know that you are a Conveyor? Like the airplane, anywhere you land, people will come to you for their luggage (blessings). The barren passengers will carry their bags of fruitfulness from you. Sinners will collect their suitcases of salvation from you. Sick passengers will come to you for their baggage of healing or divine health. The poor will look for you for their handbags of wealth and prosperity. The downcast will make their ways to the Conveyor (you) for their big bags of comfort. You certainly carry everybody's requirement! You are a Conveyor!

Let me blow your mind. Are you aware that passengers with dead relatives will look for you for their luggage of resurrection? Can you now understand who you are? If your mind is not blown yet, then, let me shatter it. You, yes, you are a Conveyor of God!

Go Shopping

1 Kings 18:41 - And Elijah said unto Ahab, Get thee up, eat and drink; for there is a sound of abundance of rain.

In the old agrarian African villages, whenever the planting season is over, farmers usually go and strengthen their barns. Those that do not have barns will go and build new ones.

In modern societies throughout the world, once a woman visits a doctor and confirms that she is pregnant (especially the first child), she will start shopping for baby things.

Brethren, I don't know what you might have asked the Lord to do for you, I don't know what seed you have sown, but the Holy Spirit has asked me to tell you to start strengthening your barns (build new barns if need be), start shopping for your prophetic babies, for I hear the sound of abundance of rain! Your harvest is breaking forth, your barrenness is reversed, and your drought is over in Jesus Name.

Amen.

The Hotter the Better

He spoke and commanded that they heat the furnace seven times more than it was usually heated – Daniel 3:19b

Nothing could stop Joseph's dream from coming to pass because it came from God. Throwing him into a pit, selling him into slavery, false accusation, putting him in prison, etc could not.

Brethren, as co-heirs with Christ Jesus, just be prepared because weapons would certainly be formed against you (Isaiah 54:17), enemies will surely gather to destroy you, you will surely be persecuted and God will not stop them. But we know the end of the matter. Don't we?.

In South Africa, Coal and Diamond come from the same source and are similarly useless in their natural state. But test them with fire and you will see the difference! While Coal becomes useless after passing through the fire, the beauty and glory of Diamonds shine brighter with more heat! One more thing, it is actually the heat from Coal that is used to bring out the qualities of Diamonds!

Your enemies and distracters, instead of becoming your stumbling blocks are going to be the stepping-stones to your glory!

Let them bring on the heat.

Jesus Christ in Hell

Matthew 12:29 - Or else how can one enter into a strong man's house, and spoil his goods, except he first bind the strong man? and then he will spoil his house.

One of the ways Satan tempted Jesus was to try and make Him bow to him. (Matthew 4:9 And saith unto him, All these things will I give thee, if thou wilt fall down and worship me).

Shortly after that encounter, Jesus Christ was in hell, Satan's domain (dwelling place). This time, the devil (who was fully armed and ready for battle) wasn't tempting or deceiving; he commanded his demons and angels to force Jesus to bow to him!

The Bible records that Jesus Christ didn't just refuse to bow, but having spoiled principalities and powers, he made a

shew of them openly, triumphing over them in it (Colossians 2:15).

What do you think happened to Satan's armour? Jesus Christ didn't just take them away from the devil, He first bound him before spoiling everything the devil had!

Luke 11:22 - But when a stronger than he shall come upon him, and overcome him, he taketh from him all his armour wherein he trusted, and divideth his spoils.

Mark 3:27 - No man can enter into a strong man's house, and spoil his goods, except he will first bind the strong man; and then he will spoil his house.

Brethren, Satan has no power! He only deceives those who are not aware of the disgraceful way he was stripped of his powers!

All Protocols Observed

If any Head of State or President sends a Permanent Secretary or even a more junior person to represent him at any occasion, the person will be seated at the centre of the high table and will be accorded all honour, privileges and authority before any other person present, be it the Governor of a State, the Vice President, or any other government official.

Saints of God, Jesus Christ did not bring religion to the world, He brought a Kingdom. There is no kingdom without a territory, authority and order (protocols). That Kingdom Jesus prayed the Father to bring is now come!

You and I (all born again children of God) are representatives of that Kingdom whose ruler is the King of Kings and the Lord of Lords! In any occasion and in any situation where we find ourselves, for all protocols to be properly observed, we must be seated at the centre of that situation and occasion, we must be accorded all privileges and authorities due to the One we represent – the Lord Jesus Christ! One more thing, our Kingdom supersedes every other kingdom (including the system of this world whose ruler is satan the devil).

You may not know how powerful you are, but keep reigning!

Focus

When Gideon was going to fight the Midianites, God had to reduce the number of men Gideon used in executing the war. What strategy did God use? He first eliminated those that exhibited fear. The second thing was focus. All the people that bowed their heads to the water were rejected by God. The ones that lapped water, putting their hands to their mouths (because they wanted to keep their eyes on their enemies) were chosen.

God has not and cannot change! You cannot be used by God if you are a fearful person. You cannot be used by God if you keep your eyes away from soul-winning which is actually the summary of Christianity.

Whether you are witnessing one-on-one, door-to-door, funding nationwide crusades and evangelism or financing the satellite transmission of the gospel worldwide, keep at it, don't be distracted and God will surely use you for His glory. Remember that His rewards are beyond description!

Judges 7:5-6 - So he brought down the people unto the water: and the LORD said unto Gideon, Every one that lappeth of the water with his tongue, as a dog lappeth, him shalt thou set by himself; likewise every one that boweth down upon his knees to drink. And the number of them that lapped, putting their hand to their mouth, were three hundred men: but all the rest of the people bowed down upon their knees to drink water.

Head or Tail, You Win!

Can you imagine a coin with the same inscriptions and marks on each side, i.e maybe, the inscription of the Queen of England? What do you think the result will be if this coin is tossed to determine the result of something important to you? Yes, you are right, head or tail you will win!

You don't have to imagine this, you can actually experience it! That is the experience of the born again child of God. Head or tail, he wins! Yes, along the way things will happen that may seem as if he is disadvantaged, but the end of the matter is what matters.

Psalm 37:37 -Mark the perfect man, and behold the upright: for the end of that man is peace.

Romans 8:28 - And we know that all things work together for good to them that love God, to them who are the called according to his purpose.

The Compass

The compass is the best directional instrument ever made by man. Compass is a navigational instrument for finding directions. Ask any sailor and he will tell you that you can never miss your way with a compass. The remarkable thing about the compass is that anywhere you keep it; it must always point to the north!

Why is that?

I found the answer in the bible! The north is the dwelling place of the Most High, Mount Zion! (Psalm 48:2 Beautiful for situation, the joy of the whole earth, is Mount Zion, on the sides of the north, the city of the great King).

The compass is like the Bible, it is the best directional book God ever produced. The Bible is the Word of God used by man to find direction for life and much more. Ask any believer and he will tell you that you can never go wrong on any decision made with the Bible. The remarkable thing about the Bible is that anywhere it is used, the same result is guaranteed!

You need your compass (I mean your Bible) if you must not miss your way!

2 Timothy 3: 16-17 - All scripture is given by inspiration of God, and is profitable for doctrine, for reproof, for correction, for instruction in righteousness: That the man of God may be perfect, thoroughly furnished unto all good works.

Same Clothes for Forty Years?

Everything made by God or man starts dying from the day they are made (no thanks to Adam). A child starts dying from the day he/she is born, i.e, from womb to tomb. Even inanimate objects- car, t.v, house, etc, starts depreciating (dying) from the day one starts to use them.

Regarding man's life, the original plan of God was for man to live without dying! Thanks be to God, through the death and resurrection of Jesus Christ, God has restored that plan. Is it possible for anything to disobey this law of death? The answer is yes! In the wilderness, God suspended the law of death on the clothes (garment, raiment) of the Israelites for forty years!

Deuteronomy 8:4 - Thy raiment waxed not old upon thee, neither did thy foot swell, these forty years.

The reason God did this is found in Romans 8:2 where the Law of Spirit of Life (which is the result of the price Jesus paid for all believers) invalidates the law of sin and death.

Romans 8:2 - For the law of the Spirit of life in Christ Jesus hath made me free from the law of sin and death.

God does not and CANNOT die! He is God! He was not made, He was not created! If God was kind enough to create us in His image (people that cannot die), you can now understand how powerful you are!

All you need is to put the Law of the Spirit of Life in action in your life and you will find out that your life and your possessions (cars, houses, children, clothes, etc) will start disobeying the law of dying (depreciating, aging, spoiling). It will take revelation to understand this message!

1 Peter 1:23 - Being born again, not of corruptible seed, but of incorruptible, by the word of God, which liveth and abideth for ever.

John 1:13 - Which were born, not of blood, nor of the will of the flesh, nor of the will of man, but of God.

Psalm 82:6 - I have said, Ye are gods; and all of you are children of the most High.

Eighteen Years

It was just like any other day
She woke up high spirited and said her prayers
Her daily chores she did as routinely as ever
The sun was setting when her world came tumbling down

She began to feel giddy for reasons unknown to her
Her body swiftly became warm, her muscles tight
Suspending her work, she eased into the nearest chair
She said a short prayer, hoping to wake up from that dream

One day turned to eighteen days
Her fears turned to distress, her distress into horror
She was bent over and could not straighten up at all
She was bound by unseen pain, caged
by unknown powers

Eighteen days turned to eighteen months
Her horror turned to nightmares
Hope started fading; faith started shaking
Tears started drying; doubt started teasing

Eighteen months turned to eighteen years
Her nightmare turned into her realities
Her life adjusted to her infirmities
She longed for solution in heaven

Then Jesus came and changed her world forever
With hands of mercy and words of grace
"Woman thou art loosed"
Those eighteen-lettered sentence
restored her eighteen years!

Take With You Words

Have you ever witnessed a scene where somebody wanted to travel to a far away land for some reasons – studies, business, marriage, etc? Did you witness the person's loved ones praying for him/her? Well, that is good and desirable, but I have found out from my Bible that there is something better than prayers of your loved ones!

There shall come situations and circumstances where these prayers may not work. There would come events and challenges in the far away land where you may not have enough time to read your Bible. What do you do in such instances?

Take with you words, and turn to the LORD (Hosea 14:2).

Why do you need to take with you words? Because if God could not make anything without the Word, you cannot accomplish anything without the same Words! (John 1:3). If it true that you were created in the image of God (Gen. 1:26), if it is true that you are a child of the Most High (Psalm 82:6), if it is true that you are born of the incorruptible seed of God (1 Peter 1:23), if it is true that you were born, not of blood, nor of the will of the flesh, nor of the will of man, but of God (John 1:13) then, like the Almighty God, you can create and recreate anything with your powerful Words!

I pray to God that you will understand what I'm trying to explain by the revelation of God! If you do, you will realize that wherever you wish to go, no matter how far, you do not need to know anybody, you do not need to have any money, you do not need to carry anything with you! Take with you Words, and turn to the LORD!!!

It may be in the belly of a fish, it may be in the den of a lion, it may be in a prison, it maybe in furnace, it does not matter, take with you Words, and turn to the LORD!!!

Mad Saints

From the world's stand point, you have to be mad to be a Christian. If like God we call things which be not as though they were (Romans 4:17) would you blame people when they call us mad?

Didn't Festus call Paul mad for his preaching? (Acts 26:24 – 25 - And as he thus proceeded with his defense, Festus called out loudly, Paul, you are mad! Your great learning is driving you insane. But Paul replied, I am not mad, most noble Festus, but I am uttering the straight, sound truth). (2 Corinthians 5:13 - For if we are beside ourselves [mad, as some say], it is for God and concerns Him; if we are in our right mind, it is for your benefit).

If we look not at the things which are seen, but at the things which are not seen: for the things which are seen are temporal; but the things which are not seen are eternal, should we not be considered mad? (2 Corinthians 4:18).

How can you say that you have evidence of things not seen and substance of things hoped for, if you are not insane? (Hebrews 11:1). But like our Daddy who framed the worlds by His word so that things which are seen were not made of things which do appear, we are happy to be the mad children of the Almighty God!

To prove to you how mad we are, no matter how terrible any sickness or disease may be to every other person, we can never say that we are sick because Isaiah 33:24 says that "And the inhabitant shall not say, I am sick".

I can go on and on, but for now, let all my fellow mad saints shout hallelujah!

Where is your umbrella?

Hebrews 11:1 - Now faith is the substance of things hoped for, the evidence of things not seen.

One day a church in America decided to pray for rain after months of intensive heat that began to affect men, animals and crops. When the final "amen" was said that fateful Sunday evening, the Pastor observed that God could have answered the prayers of only ONE member of the congregation – a small 7 years-old girl that had come with her little umbrella!

What exactly are you praying about? Where is your spiritual "umbrella"? Are you 100% convinced that God will or has answered your prayers? If so, where is the evidence of your faith?

All that Glitters

He was driving at 80 kilometres per hour. The weather was perfect. Everything was perfect and he was reflecting on how God had been so good to him and to his family.

Then, he observed from his side window, the latest Toyota Camry car speed past him. His peace and contentedness evaporated. That car represented everything he wanted in life.

The comfort of the car, the black colour, the speed, the beauty, the glory, the .... `Oh my God!!!'

Only 2 minutes ago, he was day-dreaming about it, now; the car was a total wreck, a mangled metal. If not for the air bag, the owner would have been dead!

Apparently, the car was not speeding intentionally, its brakes failed and the so-called comfort, beauty, glory, ... were the mirage of a man in desperation.

Brethren, never envy others (especially unbelievers) because their so- called successes are only but a mirage!

Psalm 37:35-37: I have seen the wicked in great power, and spreading himself like a green bay tree. Yet he passed away, and, lo, he was not: yea, I sought him, but he could not be found. Mark the perfect man, and behold the upright: for the end of that man is peace.

By this time tomorrow

Fear ye not, stand still, and see the salvation of the LORD

Israel:
Famine ravaged their city
They were in a state of pity
Bird's droppings were sold
Cannibalistic stories were told

Then the Man of God prophesied
Morrow, you'll be over-supplied
It was lepers God did choose
To spread the miraculous news

Syria:
Their city was impregnable,
their army was indomitable
Their economy was formidable
Their influence was applaudable

Then the Man of God spoke
Their economy went broke
Their mighty army fled
Leaving behind their bread

Do your challenges look formidable?
Impossible, unsubduable, indomitable?

Thus says the Lord....
Is the LORD'S hand waxed short?
Is there anything I cannot sort?
With me (God) all things are possible
With me, nothing is impossible

Quiet Time

Matthew 14:23 - And when he had sent the multitudes away, he went up into a mountain apart to pray: and when the evening was come, he was there alone.

The greatest miracles Jesus performed when He was here on earth in flesh and blood were conceived and concluded on His knees in the privacy of his solitude. The world only witnessed the signs, the wonders and the glories of the rigorous time of prayer and fellowship He had with His Father!

Brethren, I am convinced that the future belongs to us because like Jesus, our time of prayer and fellowship with our Heavenly Father with the help of the Holy Ghost will guarantee the same result!

Quiet times with God guarantees glorious times with men!

Relax: He's in Charge

1 Peter 5:7: - Casting the whole of your care all your anxieties, all your worries, all your concerns, once and for all on Him, for He cares for you affectionately and cares about you watchfully.

What do you do when there is nothing you can do to help a situation? He says that at such times, you should cast all your cares, anxieties, concerns, worries, doubts, challenges, uncertainties, helplessness, inabilities, difficulties, unfulfilled dreams and aspirations on Him for He cares for you!!!

What exactly does God do with all these worries from His children? He simply refines them. He turns anxieties into abilities, victories for worries, shouts of joy for doubts of the future, changes for challenges, rhapsodies of realities for uncertainties, hopefulness for helplessness, capabilities for inabilities, opportunities for difficulties, wings for your dreams and aspirations.

Relax, when God does not deliver, He rescues, when He does not stop your enemies from throwing you into the lion's den, He will be with you inside the den and will surely stop the mouth of the lion!!!

How Big Are Your Dreams?

Romans 8:17 - And if children, then heirs; heirs of God, and joint-heirs with Christ; if so be that we suffer with him, that we may be also glorified together.

How big, how lofty and how wild are your dreams? What are those things you wish to accomplish here on earth before meeting one-on-one with Jesus? Are they as vain as having vacations in all the continents of the world or as glorious as single-handedly sponsoring the biggest crusades in the world?

I just want to remind you that eternity has been set abroad in your heart. I want to confront you with the fact that your small dreams may be good enough for you personally but they are certainly NOT big enough for somebody who has been endued with power from on high, filled with the maximum capacity of the Holy Ghost and who is a bona fide joint-heir with Christ!!!

Junk those little dreams, jettison those mediocre desires, get rid of those mundane wishes, and take advantage of whom and whose you are!!! Your Daddy owns the world! Your partner (joint-heir means 100% joint ownership) Jesus Christ, is bigger than big!!! Nothing is too good for you!!!

Satan: The Toothless Bulldog

It was the fiercest beast he had ever seen in his life. Its weight could be comparable to a lion's. He became motionless the moment their eyes locked. The growling sound gained momentum with time. It started wagging its tail as it began to circle him. His heart beat started racing beyond control. His adrenaline and fear hormones peaked. Sweat dropped from his shaking hands. Too terrified to reason, he mopped and waited.

The beast's growling was interjected with barks. He expected an imminent attack any moment. Then, he noticed something very strange. Could he be dreaming, is he in a trance?

He observed again, very intently, very carefully. Something was missing from the beast's mouth.

The dog was indeed toothless, powerless. His confidence began to return. He clenched his fist, bit his lips. "Get out of here now" he shouted. It was instantaneous, magical. It wagged its tail and obeyed.

The devil is a toothless bulldog. He deceives only the uninformed.

Resist the devil, and he will flee from you - (James 4:7).

They were truly hemmed in !

They were truly hemmed in
The Egyptian forces charged in
From every side they marched in
Their fears were heightened
Everybody was frightened

Were there no graves in Egypt?
Why did you take us out of Egypt?
Why perish here in a wilderness?
Where is your God's kindness?
Stand still and see God's salvation!

The winds and the waves raged
Within the boat they were caged
The weather became very boisterous
They never saw nature so dangerous

Master, careth not that we perish?
Sleeping soundly without worry
Our situation don't you cherish?
Do something, Master, hurry
He woke and calmed the sea and the
waves

What has hemmed you in?
What forces are against you?
Do enemies and problems rage?
Stand still and you will see His
salvation!

Same River:
Different Paradigms

Colossians 2:9 - For in him dwelleth all the fulness of the Godhead bodily.

Here was Moses and millions of Israelites hemmed in (sandwiched) between the mighty Egyptian army and the mighty Red Sea. Moses almost panicked, but God told him to divide the Red Sea himself and he did.

Here was Joshua and the millions of Israelites hemmed in between enemy forces and the River Jordan. He remembered Moses and the Red Sea. As the feet of the priests that carried the Ark of God touched the river, it parted.

Here was Elijah and his servant, Elisha. Elijah was on his way to eternal transportation unto glory, but, the Jordan River was a hindrance. He remembered Moses and Joshua. With his mantle, he divided the River.
Here was Elisha, alone with Elijah's mantle. He needed to go back

across the Jordan. He evoked the powers he just received from the mantle and parted the Jordan River.

Fast Forward: Here was Jesus, in whom dwelleth the fullness of God bodily. He needed to join His disciples. But, in front of Him was the same Jordan River. There was a paradigm shift. He neither remembered Moses and the Red Sea nor Joshua, Elijah or Elisha and the Jordan.

He refused to recognise the River and walked on it!!!!
Hear me; your parents may have struggled to raise you. You may be struggling to raise your family. You may be working things out gradually with great expectations for the future.

There should be a paradigm shift! Your future should look nothing like your past! You are going to own houses you did not build! You are going to own companies and corporations where you once worked!

You are going to have unending streams of income! You are going to be consulted by nations and international organisations! The biggest things in this world are going to be done by you!

How? Through the same mechanization, transportation and manifestation that caused Jesus to walk on the waters His forbearers divided!

Brain Washed?

John 2:5: His mother saith unto the servants, Whatsoever he saith unto you, do it.

Jesus brain washed His disciples for about three years during which time they lost their thinking faculties.

Think about it, if you were asked to go to a stream and catch a fish and bring out a coin to use and pay tax, would you do it? Wouldn't that instruction seem ridiculous to you?

If you were asked to pour dish water in cups and serve them to dignitaries at a serious occasion would you do it?

If you were asked to go and untie a colt that belongs to somebody else and just reply that "the Lord needs it" if you were asked by their owners, would you do it knowing that you could be stoned for stealing?

If you were asked to serve small pieces of bread and fish to multitudes of people, wouldn't you mind the ridiculous instruction?

If you were asked to fish on disturbed water, against your expert knowledge, would you do it?

Yet, the disciples of Jesus carried out these seemingly "foolish instructions" and from those training, they became miracle workers.

Those things the Holy Spirit is asking you to do today, do they sound stupid? Do they seem funny and ridiculous? Will you go ahead and do them?

Hibernating Prophecies

Daniel 9:2 - In the first year of his reign I Daniel understood by books the number of the years, whereof the word of the LORD came to Jeremiah the prophet, that he would accomplish seventy years in the desolations of Jerusalem.

Like a computer that's not in use, the Words of God, especially prophesies, hibernate (lie dormant) until they are acted upon. God's promise to the children of Israel was hibernating and the people of Israel could have remained in exile if Daniel had not studied and discovered the set time for their liberation and interceded for the whole nation.

Isaiah, Jeremiah and the other prophets wrote so many things about Jesus. These prophesies were hibernating for so many years until Jesus Christ, very studious, appeared on the scene and acted upon them in the volume of books that were written about Him.

Who knows how many prophesies have been spoken about and concerning you. Who knows how many of them are just hibernating, waiting for you to discover and act upon them!

The effort required from you is as simple as just touching any keyboard of your computer which will turn the hibernation to active mode! The Word of God does not need or require any assistance from anybody, only faith puts it in an active mode!

Evil Men Are Out There Working For You!

It is 5: 30 in the morning. The day is breaking here in Lagos. This second most populous city in Africa (after Cairo, Egypt) is gradually bustling with activities. Traffic is building up and the streets are coming to life.

Many of the people who are working very hard and tracking deals everywhere are not even aware that they are fulfilling Scriptures.

They are working so hard, gathering and heaping this wealth for the Christians. Yes, you and I!

Do not be surprised, whether it is God that is giving them the wealth or not, they are multiplying them (with sweat, sorrow and pain) for the righteous!

Job 27:13;16-17 - This is the portion of a wicked man with God, and the heritage of oppressors, which they shall receive of the Almighty. Though he heap up silver as the dust, and prepare raiment as the clay; He may prepare it, but the just shall put it on, and the innocent shall divide the silver.

Ecclesiastes 2:26 - For God giveth to a man that is good in his sight wisdom, and knowledge, and joy: but to the sinner he giveth travail, to gather and to heap up, that he may give to him that is good before God. This also is vanity and vexation of spirit.

Isn't it so glorious that apart from our own efforts, God has sent out the wicked man out on the streets today to make wealth for us? I am yet to get over the fact that as Christians, we are meant to reap where we do not sow!!!

The Obama in All of Us

Romans 4:18 - Who against hope believed in hope, that he might become the father of many nations, according to that which was spoken, So shall thy seed be.

The election of Barack Obama is very significant in so many ways, but, I will restrict myself to the implication for Christians. There is an Obama in all of us.

Barack Obama came from nowhere to become the most powerful man on earth. How did he achieve that in such a short time?

The audacity of his hope, the tenacity of his faith, the sagacity of his choices, the indomitability of his dreams, and the veracity of his belief are the combination of what helped him. He shares many of these traits with great members of our family:

Abraham had the same audacity of hope (Romans 4:18). Daniel, Shadrach, Meshach, and Abednego had the same tenacity of faith (Daniel 3:17). So did David (1 Samuel 17:49). He shares the same indomitability of dream with Joseph (Genesis 41:41). He shares the same veracity of belief with Paul (Acts 21: 13). He shares the same sagacity of choices with Solomon (1 kings 4:30).

Are people complaining that your dreams are too high? That your desires are too wild? That your hopes and aspirations are too audacious? That your faith in this your God is excessive? Point them to Barack Obama!

Those lofty desires inside your heart represent the Obama in you. All you need is to say, just like Obama did – YES I CAN!

Illegal Occupants

Exodus 3:17 - And I have said, I will bring you up out of the affliction of Egypt unto the land of the Canaanites, and the Hittites, and the Amorites, and the Perizzites, and the Hivites, and the Jebusites, unto a land flowing with milk and honey.

When God gave the above mentioned lands to the Israelites, He did not negotiate with nor inform the occupants. In fact, as far as these people were concerned, nothing changed and they were still engrossed in their daily activities until the fullness of time.

As far as God was concerned, there was only one King in Israel as soon as Samuel anointed David as the king of Israel when he was less than 17 years. Saul `illegally' occupied the throne for 13 years before David finally assumed his rightful Kingship.

What I'm trying to tell you beloved of God, is that it does not matter who is `illegally' occupying your business today. God does not need to inform them that He has delivered their businesses to you!

Milk and Honey, Silver and Gold, the Forces of the Gentiles, the Abundance of the Sea, indeed all the things that pertain to life and godliness have been delivered to you and with the help of the Holy Ghost, you will begin to occupy till He comes!

Was Jesus Unfair to The Fig Tree?

Was Jesus unfair to the fig tree that He cursed which died the next day? It was not the season for the fig tree to bear fruit, so, why was Jesus upset?

Mark 11:13 - Seeing in the distance a fig tree in leaf, he went to find out if it had any fruit. When he reached it, he found nothing but leaves, because it was not the season for figs.

Jesus was upset because, there is no seasonality in spirituality. There is nothing natural about God or His desires. That was why a fish could yield out a legal tender – coin. That was why dish water could turn to wine.

Why is this important? As believers, you are expected to reap from where you do not sow! Your harvest should not be limited by times and seasons! Your prosperity is divine and should be spiritually produced.

Jeremiah 17:8 For he shall be as a tree planted by the waters, and that spreadeth out her roots by the river, and shall not see when heat cometh, but her leaf shall be green; and shall not be careful in the year of drought, neither shall cease from yielding fruit.

Executive Privilege

John 16:13- Howbeit when he, the Spirit of truth, is come, he will guide you into all truth: for he shall not speak of himself; but whatsoever he shall hear, that shall he speak: and he will shew you things to come.

Have you ever noticed that as a matter of executive protocol everybody that walks with the president of a country always make sure that they are at least a few steps behind the president –his aides, protocol officers, advisers, ministers, etc.

It is called executive privilege. I have also noticed that spiritually, the greatest Christians are those that give the Holy Spirit of God executive privilege. Those that allow the Holy Spirit of God to be a few steps ahead of them never make mistakes, never make wrong decisions and never say or do anything wrong because He (the Holy Spirit) is their guide.

Is the Holy Spirit enjoying executive privilege in your life and affairs?

Economic Solution to Poverty According to Jesus

Luke 7:22 - Then Jesus answering said unto them, Go your way, and tell John what things ye have seen and heard; how that the blind see, the lame walk, the lepers are cleansed, the deaf hear, the dead are raised, to the poor the gospel is preached.

Isn't it remarkable that Jesus Christ's solution to poverty is the gospel, not silver, not gold, not handouts? The reason is because any other help a poor man receives will be temporary. The permanent solution to poverty according to Jesus is the gospel!

How? Joshua 1:8 and Psalm 1:3 link sustainable prosperity to meditation and practice of the Word of God. It may be difficult for a poor man to actually see the relationship between doing God's word and breaking away from the shackles of penury, but, since we can never be wiser than Jesus Christ, there is no need beating around the bush, the gospel is the answer to poverty!

Deuteronomy 8:18 But thou shalt remember the LORD thy God: for it is he that giveth thee power to get wealth, that he may establish his covenant which he sware unto thy fathers, as it is this day.

Whosoever Is Born Of God Doth Not Commit Sin

Sickle cell anemia is an inherited, lifelong condition. People who have sickle cell anemia are born with it. It is predominantly a disease associated with black people. It is almost genetically impossible for Caucasians to suffer from this sickle cell problem. That's just how it is. Medical science is still battling to find out why this situation is this way. Yet, millions die yearly around the world as a result of that ailment.

If you can understand this, it will help you understand it perfectly when John wrote that whoever is born of God does not commit sin. It is not genetically possible for a born again child of God to sin. Love does not permit him to. Love for God and love for people. In the unlikely event he transgresses (go against God's word), the Spirit of God within him causes him to repent and he is automatically forgiven.

1 John 3:9 Whosoever is born of God doth not commit sin; for his seed remaineth in him: and he cannot sin, because he is born of God.

Sin is a nature thing, not an act thing. An unbeliever cannot but sin because his nature makes it impossible for him to do right. He lies, fornicates, steals, kills and generally sins because that's his nature.

A believer, whom God's love has been shared abroad in his heart, cannot sin. His nature does not permit him to.

More Than a Story

He was young and energetic. He loved stories and listened intently when he heard stories, especially, the ones that talked about Jehovah and His awesome wonders. He heard about Abraham, Isaac and Jacob and God's relationship with them. He was told of Joseph, his dreams and sojourn in Egypt.

He marveled particularly at the story of Moses and how God through him, parted the mighty Red Sea. He was thrilled that Joshua could command the sun to stand still for God's children to execute their war. In Jericho, etc.

As a rustic shepherd boy, he was proving these awesome stories daily in the solitude of the wilderness. He used that awesome name of Jehovah to wrestle and kill a lion and a bear, and true to what he was told, God kept on working mighty miracles with him out there in the lonely mountains and planes of his village.

One day, he was terribly shocked to see the same people that told him beautiful stories of the mighty acts of God cowering at the presence of a mere philistine giant called Goliath and his four brothers.

He couldn't stand it. No, not with all he had heard and experienced.... You know the rest of the story...

Brothers and sisters, do you truly believe the Bible? Is it a book filled with fairy tales? Have you ever experienced the awesome act of God before? If yes, why do you now cower at some situations and circumstances? Is there anything too much for God?

Philippians 4:6 - Be careful for nothing; but in every thing by prayer and supplication with thanksgiving let your requests be made known unto God.

Your Set Time Has Come!

Daniel 2:21 And he changeth the times and the seasons: he removeth kings, and setteth up kings: he giveth wisdom unto the wise, and knowledge to them that know understanding

Thou shalt arise, and have mercy upon Zion: for the time to favour her, yea, the set time, is come (Psalm 102:13).

He was just a mad man in the lonely mountains of the country of the Gadarenes. He was filled with unclean spirit, wild and uncontrollable. The graveyard was his dwelling place. He inflicted heavy wounds on himself at the bidding of the evil spirits that held him captive.

BUT, when his season collided with his time, when the time to favor him, yea, the set time was come, Jesus suspended His busy schedule and abandoned the whole world and came specifically for him!!! I am sure you know the rest of the story...

That same Jesus is telling you today that your season and your time have merged; the time to favor you, yea, the set time has come. His full attention is specifically focused on you today.

Beyond yourself, beyond your faith, beyond your senses, beyond principalities and powers, beyond any imaginable force in heaven, on earth and beneath the earth, your blessings can no longer be stopped!!! It's just too late now!!!

You may never know why and how, but, it is your set (appointed) time for an unending harvest of miracles. Whether you believe it or not, it will surely happen because the Lord Himself has said so.

The Sufferings Of Christ, And The Glory That Should Follow

1 Peter 1: 11 – Searching what, or what manner of time the spirit of Christ which was in them did signify, when it testified beforehand the sufferings of Christ, and the glory that should follow.

The above scripture explains that glory should of necessity follow the sufferings of Christ. So why are you still suffering what Christ had already suffered? Is your suffering bringing glory to God? Think about it!

Overnight Success

There are many exams in the world today that if you pass them very well (i.e if you are amongst the best ten worldwide) you will have instant scholarship to the best schools in the world. GRE® - Graduate Record Examinations®, Graduate Management Admission Test (GMAT), and a host of Information Technology exams are a few examples.

For you to achieve this feat (no matter how intelligent you may be), you must study to a point that you will be dripping with knowledge of that area of study. If you sacrifice your time and study, you are guaranteed of instant (overnight) success as some of the scholarships you might get run into thousands of dollars. In addition, the best companies in the world will be waiting for your graduation to offer you mind-blowing jobs.

Great as this may sound, the bible records that the only success that truly matters is good success and the modus operandi on how to acquire this good success is found in Joshua 1:8.

Matthew 19:20 tells an interesting story of somebody that practiced Joshua 1:8 and of course turned out wealthy!

What do you desire? Overnight success or good success?

Showcase

Hebrews 1:3 - Who being the brightness of his glory, and the express image of his person.

Marketers use showcases to display their best products. Jewelleries, fast foods, personal effects, clothes, cars, what have you.

God also showcases his best products (you and I) to the devil and the entire world. I'll prove it from the bible. God showcased Job and Jesus!

Job 1:8 - And the LORD said unto Satan, Hast thou considered my servant Job, that there is none like him in the earth, a perfect and an upright man, one that feareth God, and escheweth evil?

Matthew 3:17 - And lo a voice from heaven, saying, This is my beloved Son, in whom I am well pleased.*

Like fresh bread from the oven of the Holy Spirit, like a perfect work of art crafted and framed by Jesus Christ Himself, as an effulgence of the glory of God Almighty, God is through with you, He has displayed you in His awesome showcase!!! Why am I so sure?

Because Ephesians 2:10 says that "For we are his workmanship, created in Christ Jesus unto good works, which God hath before ordained that we should walk in them".

When people are talking about you, when you attract envy and jealousy, please don't blame the people; just know and remember that you are on display in God's showcase!!!

Who Told You That You Were Naked

2 Corinthians 5:7 (For we walk by faith, not by sight:)

The consequence of the first sin committed by man was that man stopped relating to God spiritually but started using his physical senses which was why God asked Adam and Eve who told them they were naked.

Genesis 3:11 - And he said, Who told thee that thou wast naked? Hast thou eaten of the tree, whereof I commanded thee that thou shouldest not eat?

God is still asking you and I the same question:

Acts 29:1 - And he (God) said, Who told thee (Michael Ogbaa) that thou art not a billionaire? Hast thou been walking by your senses (sight) and not by faith, whereof I commanded thee?

Brethren, there is no limitations with God, we are the ones that limit ourselves by choice!
Parting question: Didn't God know Adam and Eve were naked?

Hannah Talks to God

Dear God of Hosts

Why has thou shut up my womb? Why has thou allowed my adversary to provoke me sore? Right now, weeping is my potion and I hardly eat. I am indeed in bitterness of soul.

Dear Hannah,

You should know better than associate me with evil. You are not only inscribed in the palms of my hands, the thoughts I have for you are good, not evil. Hannah, forever and a day, you are the apple of my eyes. In time you will know that all things will work together for your good. Do you not know that the trying of your faith worketh patience?

O LORD of hosts

If thou wilt indeed look on the affliction of thine handmaid, and remember me, and not forget thine handmaid, but wilt give unto thine handmaid a man child. Then I will give him unto the LORD all the days of his life, and there shall no razor come upon his head. I am a woman of a sorrowful spirit. I have poured out my soul before thee my LORD. Out of the abundance of my complaint and grief have I spoken.

Dear Hannah,

I have heard your prayer and seen your contrite heart. Let me explain why it took a while for me to answer thee. You were looking for a male child, but I was looking for the mother of my first prophet. One that will anoint my first king for my people Israel. The one that will anoint the grandfather of my Son Jesus. Because of your vow, I have chosen you to be the one. Generations shall hear of thy faith and be blessed.

Brethren, delay (when it comes to God) is not denial. God is planning something big for you!!! Keep believing!!!

Impossicant

Daniel 2:20-22 - Blessed be the name of God for ever and ever: for wisdom and might are his: And he changeth the times and the seasons: he removeth kings, and setteth up kings: he giveth wisdom unto the wise, and knowledge to them that know understanding: He revealeth the deep and secret things: he knoweth what is in the darkness, and the light dwelleth with him.

My course mate in university used to use the word "impossicant" to define anything he believed was impossibly impossible. In the Bible, when King Nebuchadnezzar asked his magicians and advisors to tell him his dream and its interpretation, they replied him that it was impossicant!

Daniel 2:10 His advisors explained, " Your Majesty (Nebuchadnezzar), you are demanding the impossible! No king, not even the most famous and powerful, has ever ordered his advisors, magicians, or wise men to do such a thing. [11] It can't be done, except by the gods, and they don't live here on earth."

But there was a man called Daniel (the wisest person that lived before Solomon) who knew that the word "impossible" does not have any connection with the God of heaven! Here is his answer to the same request of King Nebuchadnezzar.

Daniel 2: 27 - Daniel answered: Your Majesty, not even the smartest person in all the world can do what you are demanding. But the God who rules from heaven can explain mysteries.

You know the rest of the story. But, do you know that when king Nebuchadnezzar became an animal and was living in the bush for 7 years it was Daniel who ruled over the kingdom before King Nebuchadnezzar recovered and was restored?

Show Me the Graveyard

The graveyard maybe be solemn
Tombs maybe arranged in columns
Filled with dead dreams and visions
Killed by dread and indecisions

Show me where you laid them
A Friend wants to trade them
Says though they be dead, yet shall they live
Says He is the resurrection, and the life

Says He need only say two words
Says "Come forth" are those words
Says you may be from any region
Says you can ask Lazarus and Legion

*John 11:44 - And he that was dead came forth, bound hand
and foot with graveclothes: and his face was bound about
with a napkin. Jesus saith unto them, Loose him, and let him
go.*

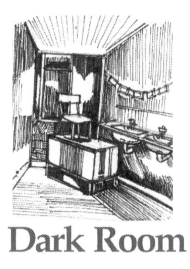

Dark Room

Romans 8:19 For the earnest expectation of the creature waiteth for the manifestation of the sons of God.

Before the advent of digital cameras, every photographer knew about the "dark room" where the negatives of their photos are processed. During this dark period, these negatives are treated with chemical solutions that make their outcome to stand the test of time. The photos are truly glorious when they come out and are displayed anywhere and everywhere.

It seems that some of us are actually in our spiritual "dark rooms" presently; the negative things in our lives are currently receiving supernatural solutions from the Holy Ghost! Our outcome will surely stand the test of time. We are going to be gloriously displayed by God anywhere and everywhere!

One final thought: remember that there was a time Polaroid cameras were the toast of everybody because they produced "wait and take" photos? People lost interest in them because, though they produce photos fast, their products start fading immediately because they never go through a dark room!

Rejoice if you are in a "dark room"!!!

The Lift

Psalm 55:22 - Cast thy burden upon the LORD, and he shall sustain thee: he shall never suffer the righteous to be moved.

As I entered the lift to my office one morning, the Holy Spirit ministered to me. I was carrying my laptop on my shoulder inside the lift. It was still as heavy on me as it was before I entered the lift. If I had dropped it, the lift could have stresslessly carried my load and I!

The Holy Spirit ministered to me that what I just observed is what happens to many Christians – they still carry their burden themselves when God can easily take care of both them and whatsoever heavy burden they come to Him with!

Brethren, let's cast all our cares upon Him for He cares for us.

Philippians 4:6 - Be careful for nothing; but in every thing by prayer and supplication with thanksgiving let your requests be made known unto God.

Mary Magdalene

Luke 8:2-3 - And certain women, which had been healed of evil spirits and infirmities, Mary called Magdalene, out of whom went seven devils, And Joanna the wife of Chuza Herod's steward, and Susanna, and many others, which ministered unto him of their substance.

Mary Magdalene is one of the disciples of Jesus that inspires me most. Immediately Jesus casted out demons from her and healed her, she became fervent and was first in so many things. I am not sure that anybody gave more money than her to the ministry of Jesus. She was the first and only person to visit the tomb of Jesus after He was buried. She was the one that broadcasted the glorious resurrection news to the whole world!!!

Let's keep informing sinners, that it does not matter how bad their sins can be (even if they have seven devils), they can be used by God more than present day pastors and church leaders.

John 20:1 - The first day of the week cometh Mary Magdalene early, when it was yet dark, unto the sepulchre, and seeth the stone taken away from the sepulchre.

Reflex Action

Psalm 62:11 - God hath spoken once; twice have I heard this; that power belongeth unto God.

Reflex action is defined as a response, often involuntary, resulting from the passage of excitation potential from a receptor to a muscle or gland, over a reflex arc. An involuntary physiological response to a stimulus. An unlearned or instinctive response to a stimulus. Footballers (including goalkeepers) with the sharpest reflexes receive the highest pay. Mohammed Ali is the most celebrated boxer of our time because of his reflexes.

It follows reason to assume that if reflex action exists in the natural, it must also exist in the spiritual. The bible is rife with people with amazing sharp spiritual reflexes, who heard and acted on the smallest and simplest instructions from God without reasoning out such instructions.

Abraham, Moses, David, Solomon, King Hezekiah, Paul, Peter, (let's not talk about Jesus because He didn't have reflexes, He was reflex action personified) etc. Joshua trained his spiritual reflexes so well that at a point, he was ready to kill an Angel of the Lord (he had even drawn his sword). At another point, he commanded the sun to stand still without thinking about it, without praying about it, and the sun actually stood still!!!

How sharp are your spiritual reflexes? How quick do you hear from and act on the Word of God?

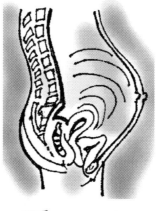

Placenta

Colossians 3:3 - For ye are dead, and your life is hid with Christ in God.

God is awesome; he hides an unborn child within the comforts of the mother's womb, covers it with a placenta and encapsulates it in a water bag. For nine months, the baby lives comfortably within this secured environment provided by God.

God is awesome; he hides his spiritual children within the comforts of the Holy Ghost, covers them with the Word of God, and encapsulates them in God Himself. For as long as they are in this sinful world, believers live comfortably within the secured environment provided by God.

We are indeed hidden in Christ in God.

John 15:19 - If ye were of the world, the world would love his own: but because ye are not of the world, but I have chosen you out of the world, therefore the world hateth you.

Armies of Israel

Goliath defiled the army of Israel whose commander-in-chief was Saul the king. Goliath was physically intimidating and loud-mouthed. He used these two advantages to put fear in the Israelites.

David knew from stories that there was another Army in Israel whose Commander-in- chief was Jehovah the Most High. In fact, by the sheer innumerable number of this army, he called it the Armies of Israel!!! He knew that these armies were indomitable. All he needed was to have them fight with him. You know the rest of the story.

Brethren, I never read anywhere in the Bible (from Genesis to Revelation) where God disbanded the Armies of (new Israel). Are you about going to war against any principality or power or evil forces of any kind? Why not go with the Armies of God?

Keep winning.

Faith at Its Finest

Hebrews 11:17 - By faith Abraham, when he was tried, offered up Isaac: and he that had received the promises offered up his only begotten son.

Every single day for 25 years, Abraham believed in the promise of God. He acted his faith by changing his name. When the physical manifestation of that promise came to pass, he had Isaac.

Then, God asked Abraham for Isaac, his greatest possession, his link to the other promises of God. Abraham did four things that displayed faith at its finest:

He set out early to sacrifice Isaac - we should be prompt to do the word of God. He didn't discuss with anybody, including his wife Sarah -- the word of God is not negotiable. He travelled for 3 days, enough time to change his mind if he wanted -- God will always test our faith with enough time to either obey or disobey Him.

Finally, as far as God was concerned (God sees from the spiritual realm), Abraham actually sacrificed Isaac. Read Hebrews 11:17-18.

Brothers and Sisters, God is not asking you for Isaac, but you are the only one that knows what He is demanding from you, can you display faith at its finest?

Jesus Wept a Second Time

John 11:35 - Jesus wept.

I used to think that Jesus only wept once as contained in the opening verse. I was wrong. Luke 19:41 shows another occasion where Jesus wept.

What made the King of Glory weep? Jesus could not have wept for Lazarus's death when He was going to resurrect him. He only wept for people's unbelief.

Jesus wept in Luke 19:41 because the inhabitants of Jerusalem refused to recognize the time of their visitation.

If Jesus was to walk the streets of the world today, He would have still be weeping because even though He has given us power over the world and told us that all things are possible to them that believe, even though He has sent us the Holy Spirit to assist us accomplish any and every thing we desire, many are still unbelieving and powerless. The Holy Spirit does not only visit but lives in us, yet, many still do not recognize the time of their visitation!

Luke 19:41-42 - And he answered and said unto them, I tell you that, if these should hold their peace, the stones would immediately cry out. And when he was come near, he beheld the city, and wept over it, Saying, If thou hadst known, even thou, at least in this thy day, the things which belong unto thy peace! but now they are hid from thine eyes

My Lord & I

Matthew 19:29 - And every one that hath forsaken houses, or brethren, or sisters, or father, or mother, or wife, or children, or lands, for my name's sake, shall receive an hundredfold, and shall inherit everlasting life.

I used to have wild dreams when I was younger; of how to build a dynasty, with few kids in the best schools in the world, with parents I will spoil with care, of having the best things life could ever offer, etc…

Then I met Jesus. He told me that he was going to give me a new dream. I asked Him if it was going to be as lofty as mine. He said no. The dream He had for me was simple… to win souls and sponsor the gospel worldwide.
"What will happen to my kids and their education, my dynasty, my parents, the best things life could offer"? His answer broke my heart and has kept me a Christian ever since…

"Michael, why do you worry about perishable things when I can give you possessions of eternal value? No plan, no dream, no vision of yours can be half as good as my desires for you. Seek ye first my kingdom and all its righteousness, and hold me accountable for all your tomorrows"…

Crucified With Christ

It was a very trying time for Nigeria. Miss World Beauty Competition was cancelled and relocated to London. An editor with Thisday Newspaper (a leading Nigerian daily newspaper) was being hunted for insulting Muslims and their office in Abuja (the capital of Nigeria) was burnt.

Lionel Peterson (of Rejoice Africa fame), Ron Kenoly and Kirk Franklin were also visiting Nigeria that same month.

There were thousands of us packed inside the main bowl of the National Stadium that night. Lionel Peterson and Ron Kenoly took us into the third heavens with soul inspiring gospel songs.

Then came Kirk Franklin. Before he started performing, he made a statement that has remained indelible in my spirit till today.

He said that when he was embarking on the trip to Nigeria, his fans and loved ones begged him not to come to Nigeria. That people were dying of diseases and others were being killed, and that there was general unrest in that land. His answer was that "you can't kill a dead man, I am crucified with Christ: nevertheless I live; yet not I, but Christ liveth in me: and the life which I now live in the flesh I live by the faith of the Son of God, who loved me, and gave himself for me (Galatians 2:20).

Awesome faith, awesome revelation, awesome boldness!

Has it dawned on your spirit that you are crucified with Christ?

I'll Rather Be Mad!

Psychologists will tell you that one of the first symptoms of insanity (madness) is talking to oneself. A close observation of insane folks will prove this point.

There are another set of mad people I know who talk to themselves.

In Genesis, the bible records that Adam and Eve heard the voice of God walking in the cool of the day. This voice which took up flesh years later to become Jesus Christ never ceased from talking…. He spoke to fish and bread, water and wave, tree and sicknesses as if they were human beings.

The woman with the issue of blood talked to herself and that "symptom of madness" got her healed by touching Jesus when everything else had failed!!!

What issues do you have? What are you talking to yourself about? Does your voice walk in the heat of the day and the cool of the night? Do you talk to your job, your car, your wallet, your money, your house, your furniture, your clothes, etc?

I rather be a mad believer than an unbelieving psychologist!

I Don't Know

I don't know what happens between the time a seed is sown and the time it germinates.

I don't know how bones are formed in a pregnant woman's womb but she delivers a baby in nine months.

I don't know where the sun hides all night and where the moon hides all day, but they will surely complete their courses every day.

I don't know what happened between the first and the six times Naaman dipped himself in the Jordan River, but, I know what happened at the seventh time.

I don't know what happened between the first and the sixth times Elijah's assistant went to observe if the rain was coming, but I know what happened on the seventh time.

I don't know what you may be waiting on God for, but I know that if God has promised it, it must surely come to pass!!! Remember, in His (God's) time, He makes all things beautiful.

Ecclesiastes 3:11 He hath made every thing beautiful in his time: also he hath set the world in their heart, so that no man can find out the work that God maketh from the beginning to the end.

Don't Stop Talking

Ephesians 6:17 - And take the helmet of salvation, and the sword of the Spirit, which is the word of God.

The bible says that the devil throws wiles and fiery darts at Christians. Wile is defined as a stratagem or trick intended to deceive or ensnare. Dart on the other hand denotes slender, pointed missile, often having tail fins, thrown by hand, shot from a blowgun, or expelled by an exploding bomb. It also connotes the stinger of an insect.

Of all the weapons the bible mentioned in Ephesians 6 as part of the whole armour of God, only the sword is an offensive weapon. The others -- breastplate, shield, and helmet are defensive weapons against the wiles of the devil.

A sword is a cutting or thrusting weapon with a long blade. If the sword of the spirit is the Word of God, then, like the physical sword, we need to go to the devil's territory with word of God... David attacked Goliath with words before charging on him! Jesus went to hell and spoiled Satan and his demons.

The best strategists know that attack is the best form of defense! In our good fight of faith, when you don't go after the devil, he will surely bombard you with wiles and fiery darts. In order to keep the devil on the run, keep talking…

The Church has been on the defensive for too long, that's why the devil has been bombarding Christians with wiles and fiery darts. But it's time we made war with the devil! (Yes, he has been defeated and we are only fighting the good fight of faith).

It's time we took the battle to the enemy's territory! Jesus defeated the devil in hell, remember?

Maybe you are about telling me, "Brother Michael, let sleeping dog lie, don't touch the tail of the lion". Pardon me, but the Devil is not a sleeping dog, he will attack you if you let him. He maybe perambulating like a lion, but the ONLY Lion of Judea is my Daddy!

In The Solitude of the Wilderness

He wanted to perfect that acoustic note with his violin. It usually never took him this long to perfect a note. He needed concentration which the serene wilderness provided him. But for the bleating of the sheep, the atmosphere was perfectly quiet and peaceful. The grass was green and the weather was glorious.

He was striking the note again when he heard that striking roar again. Yes, that was it, the reason for the distraction. He dropped the violin and concentrated on the sound. It was coming from 5 miles away. Then everywhere was dead quiet again.

He decided to write a song instead. ... "I will love thee, O LORD, my strength. The LORD is my rock, and my fortress, and my deliverer; my God, my strength, in whom I will trust; my buckler, and the horn of my salvation, and my high tower ..."

With the speed of light, it happened... the beast was coming at 30 meters per hour. It was massive, weighing about 400 pounds. Height was 10 feet horizontally and 3.5 feet vertically. All its 30 teeth were almost visible. It charged with outraged claws.

He watched as the lion snatched the first sheep it could reach, instinctively, instantaneously, he went out after it and stroke it with a sword and delivered it out of the lions mouth. The lion couldn't give up, but veraciously rose for another action, this time, against the rescuer. He caught it by its beard, and smote it with his whole might and cut it into pieces...1 Samuel 17:35.

The Day God
Danced In Heaven

Thousands of years before God commanded creation to hear the words of His Son, Jesus Christ, a man did something that made God dance in heaven with the heavenly hosts!

Joshua witnessed when God (through Moses) divided the Red Sea. He witnessed when God fed them with manna from heaven. He was there when the Lord guided them with the pillar of the cloud by day, and the pillar of fire by night. He took note when they were fed with quails from nowhere and so many other miracles.

One day, in the middle of a battle, Joshua needed the sun to stand still so that he could complete the battle. Based on his knowledge of God and what He could do, he commanded the sun to stand still!!

There was party in heaven as God gathered the angels and told them that Joshua has indeed manifested the true nature of man! That when He gave man dominion over creation, that it included the sun, the moon, and everything, and that for Joshua to have dared to use his powers, he had gladdened His heart!

Brethren, how far can you go with God? How elastic is your faith? How powerful do you believe God is?

One more thing ... Is it not amazing that because Joshua believed the limitless power of God and commanded the sun to stand still, from then till now, to the end of the world, there has and will always be a leap year. Leap years are what scientist use to round up the missing day (the day the Joshua's Miracle happened).

I'm not prophesying, but, your act of faith today (dare to believe and act on God's word today) is going to be remembered by generations yet to come!

Faith Works 100%
All The Time

Hebrews 11:1 - Now faith is the substance of things hoped for, the evidence of things not seen.

Faith is a law. Faith does not waiver. Faith is definite. There is no doubt or shadow of variability when it comes to faith. If it did not work, it was not faith because faith worked for you to have the evidence/proof/ substance of the things hoped for!

If it does not work, it is not faith! If it will not work, it certainly could not be faith. Faith always works!!!!

If a mother delivered a baby after nine months, will it not be sheer madness for anybody to come to her and say "you were not pregnant".

All she needs to do to convince that doubter is to show her baby. The baby is the proof/evidence/ substance of her pregnancy! The only problem Christians have is that they always try to show physical evidence/proof/ substance to a spiritual reality!

A thousand times no! If you doubt my faith, then, join me and come to my fourth dimension of spirit where I live and surely, you will see the evidence/proof/ substance of my faith! If you live in the third dimension where you rely on your physical senses for everything, I'm so sorry for you because you can never see my faith in action.

How can you have evidence and still doubt the thing you hoped for? Stop embarrassing faith!

Joint-Account

Ever heard of Joint Account? Ask any banker and you will understand how it works. It is an account that is usually operated by at least two people. Any money in a joint account belongs 100% to each of the operators of the account. Depending on the mandate by the operators, money can be withdrawn by any of the owners of the account by signing singly or jointly.

Are you aware that you have a joint-account with Jesus? Read your bible!!

Romans 8:17 - And if children, then heirs; heirs of God, and joint-heirs with Christ; if so be that we suffer with him, that we may be also glorified together.

The sweetest part of this story is that Jesus has given you the power of attorney to use His Name, in other words, you are the sole signatory to all the joint-accounts you have with Him!!!

What do want for yourself and for others? Healing, prosperity, children, spouse, name it, go ahead and sign that blank joint-account cheque! Jesus always funds His account!

Sweet Sweet Tomorrow

Philippians 3:13 - Brethren, I count not myself to have apprehended: but this one thing I do, forgetting those things which are behind, and reaching forth unto those things which are before.

Have you ever wondered why the front windscreen of almost every car is larger than the rear one? A pastor explained it spiritually one day and I was so blessed by his analogy: the simple reason is because your future is far greater than your past!!

Can you see why you should forget your past mistakes and glories and reach out for your sweet, sweet tomorrow?

Lay Up Gold as Dust

Have you ever travelled during a dry season with nobody left behind in your home? Did you observe how dust took over the entire home despite the shut windows and doors? Where did the dust come from?

Your prosperity and blessings this year will certainly take similar manner because Job 22:26 says that you will lay up gold as dust.

Unfortunately, this promise is not for everybody. Read Job 22: 21 27 to find out if you qualify. One important condition for laying up this gold as dust is that you must first lay up the Word of God in your heart and be a doer of it!

Then, your prosperity (like dust) will be unstoppable! The wind (which typifies the Holy Ghost) will bring blessings, favour, grace, and untold riches from Unknown and unimaginable sources!

The Other Side

Mark 4:35 - And the same day, when the even was come, he saith unto them, Let us pass over unto the other side.

Jesus once told His disciples that they should go to the other side, across the river. In between their journey, the wind and the wave became turbulent and boisterous. Jesus was deep asleep and the disciples woke Him up saying, "Master, carest thou not that we perish?" Jesus rebuked the wind and the wave.

Jesus was deep in sleep because as far as He was concerned, since He had proclaimed that they were going to the other side, it was a done-deal! (Isaiah 55:11). He couldn't understand why His disciples could not understand that.

If there is a prophecy concerning you that is yet to be fulfilled, happy are you, because you can never die till all of them come to pass!

Remote Control

Psalm 40:8 - I delight to do thy will, O my God: yea, thy law is within my heart.

I work in a Bank on Oyin Jolayemi street, in Lagos State, Nigeria. Any time I have any major problem with my computer, I contact our Adetokunbo Ademola Street, (where our IT department is located) which is about 15 minutes drive away from where I work.

They will ask me for my computer i.p address, and once I give them that, they will remotely take over my P.C. You will notice the cursor moving by itself on your computer screen as they rectify the issue.

Spiritually, when you align your will with God, and all your deeds and words are in sync with the Holy Ghost (and done in the Name of Jesus), it is akin to supplying God your i.p address!!!

He will take over and perfect the computer of your life!!!

Facts and Figures

Numbers 11:21-22 And Moses said, The people, among whom I am, are six hundred thousand footmen; and thou hast said, I will give them flesh, that they may eat a whole month. Shall the flocks and the herds be slain for them, to suffice them? or shall all the fish of the sea be gathered together for them, to suffice them?

Moses was statistically sound and mathematically gifted. He used this knowledge to question the power of the Almighty God.

God told him, "Dear Moses, you know the numbers, but it was Me that created the people you are counting. The flocks, the herds and the fish you are referring to were created by me. Why bother yourself on the strategy I will use to bring my word to pass?

Numbers 11:21 - And the LORD said unto Moses, Is the LORD'S hand waxed short? thou shalt see now whether my word shall come to pass unto thee or not.

Beloved of God, your problems cannot intimidate God, your so-called insurmountable challenges are nothing to God. You may count them one by one. They may run into thousands and millions of naira or dollars, God's answer is still the same...

Is the LORD'S hand waxed short? Is anything too hard for the LORD? Genesis 18:14

Dashboard

Ezekiel 3:21 - Nevertheless if thou warn the righteous man, that the righteous sin not, and he doth not sin, he shall surely live, because he is warned; also thou hast delivered thy soul.

Modern cars have computerized dashboards that give early warning indication of potential anomalies in cars. It could be indication of low fuel or water, overheating of the engine, unlocked doors, etc.

In the old testament of the Bible, Prophets of God acted as dashboards for the believers by warning them whenever they transgressed.

David (the man after God's heart) didn't need any dashboard because he hid the word of God in his heart! Psalm 119:11- Thy word have I hid in mine heart, that I might not sin against thee.

Then came Jesus and everything changed!!! Now, we (the beneficiaries of Jesus' sacrifice and covenant with the Father), possess something far better than a dashboard!

Imagine a car which can be able to give you early warning indication and also able to fix the anomalies while you are still driving!!! If you can imagine that, then, you truly understand the awesome power of the Holy Spirit which Jesus left with us when He ascended to Heaven!

John 14:16 - And I will ask the Father, and He will give you another Comforter (Counselor, Helper, Intercessor, Advocate, Strengthener, and Standby), that He may remain with you forever.

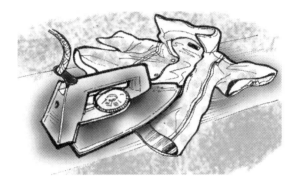

The Man and the Shirt

A man was ironing his shirt when the shirt spoke up:

Shirt: Sir, why are you trying to burn me up?

Man: No, I'm only removing the wrinkles from you

Shirt: But the heat is too much, it will soon burn me

Man: That's not possible

Shirt: Why are you so sure?

Man: Because before I began, I looked at your label and noticed the right heat for you. I do not intend to exceed that temperature
(Author Unknown)

1 Corinthians 10:13 - There hath no temptation taken you but such as is common to man: but God is faithful, who will not suffer you to be tempted above that ye are able; but will with the temptation also make a way to escape, that ye may be able to bear it.

Brethren, promotion in every area of life usually comes after examination. God follows the same principle. The first thing that happened to Jesus Christ after God proclaimed Him as His Son was temptation (examination) by the devil!

Brothers and Sisters, let's rest in this assurance: Your Maker knows you more than you know yourself and will never allow anything that is stronger than you to destroy you!

Custom-Made

Psalm 139:14 - I will praise thee; for I am fearfully and wonderfully made: marvellous are thy works; and that my soul knoweth right well.

Beloved of God,

Ask BMW, Mercedes Benz, Christian Dior, Versace, Rolex, and indeed any world class manufacturer, and they will tell you that it cost them more to produce a unique customized product. It requires more detail attention, precision and focus.

World population today is 6,609,925,096. Each one of the people that make up this number was fearfully and wonderfully crafted as master piece by the Awesome Creator Himself. All of us are custom-made, unique, with unreplicated fingerprints, vocal chords, and genetic make-up!

Ephesians 2:10 - For we are his workmanship, created in Christ Jesus unto good works, which God hath before ordained that we should walk in them.

It is indeed gratifying to know that nobody has ever existed, nobody exists today and nobody will ever exist that was/is/will be like you! That's the definition of customization!

Think About This: Can God go through this to produce sickly, poor, disadvantaged people?

Underwriters of the Gospel

Luke 8:2-3: And certain women, which had been healed of evil spirits and infirmities, Mary called Magdalene, out of whom went seven devils, And Joanna the wife of Chuza Herod's steward, and Susanna, and many others, which ministered unto him of their substance.

A lot of companies (especially banks) are raising equity funds from the capital market (both local and offshore). One thing they all have in common – First Bank, Guaranty Trust Bank, Access Bank, Oceanic Bank, Dangote Sugar, etc- is that there must be an Underwriter for the capital raising exercises to be successful.

An Underwriter is a firm that guarantees the purchase of a full issue of stocks or bonds. It is the firm that believes in the success of the stock being marketed that it writes a cheque and says that in event of the issuer of the stock or bond failing to raise the capital in question, it will fully (sometimes partly) pay!

You and I are the Underwriters of the Gospel of Jesus Christ! We are the ones that tell our Pastors… Please go ahead and preach the gospel to all mankind, in every land and every tongue, using every available means! We shall underwrite all expenses!

Read any economic or financial textbook and discover what Underwriters gain!

Read your Bible and discover what underwriters of the gospel gain!

Sabbatical Leave

The Managing Director was embarking on sabbatical leave. He had been the pioneer CEO for three years during which the company had broken every known world record in the corporate world. He wondered how the company will survive without him.

On the departure day, he handed over to Mr. Simon Peter, the erstwhile Head of Operations. He knew that Mr. Peter still needed help in running the company, so, he did two fundamental things:

Firstly, the company lawyer drafted a power of attorney nominating Mr. Simon Peter to have and execute all the powers of the MD/CEO. Secondly, he told Mr. Peter to hold on till he sends him a small pocket device that will give him direct access to him anytime, anywhere and for any situation that requires his direct input.

Two months later, Mr. Peter, new MD/CEO, with the pocket devise and the power of attorney faced a challenge that needed instantaneous action. He decided to test his power...wow, it worked!!!

Every utterance of his was law; every command carried out without fail and none of the cheques he signed was ever returned uncashed!

(if this story seems familiar to you, it is because it is actually from the bible).

Luke 24:49- And, behold, I send the promise of my Father upon you: but tarry ye in the city of Jerusalem, until ye be endued with power from on high.

Acts 1:8 - But ye shall receive power, after that the Holy Ghost is come upon you: and ye shall be witnesses unto me both in Jerusalem, and in all Judaea, and in Samaria, and unto the uttermost part of the earth.

John 14:26 - But the Comforter, which is the Holy Ghost, whom the Father will send in my name, he shall teach you all things, and bring all things to your remembrance, whatsoever I have said unto you.

Keep At It!

There was this boy in one of the remotest villages in Africa. He started practicing how to run from the age of 12. His old father was his coach and trainer. He ran from 4am to 6 pm, twice a week for several years. Oblivious to the outside world, he ran for fun and never knew that his talent could be financially rewarded.

Fastforward: here we are at the Olympic Games. The boy was amongst the long distance runners. The cameras were fixed at the current champion and the hopefuls. Nobody paid any attention to him.

When he was one lap ahead of all the other runners, commentators and journalists started asking each other who this chap was and where he came from. They searched the internet and made long distance calls to trace his history without any success.

Confession: I made up this story. Nevertheless, I was inspired to write it because of you. Whatever visions the Holy Spirit has put in your heart, keep at it, and practice from sunrise to sundown. Be focused and not distracted. Very soon, all your perspiration hatched out of your inspiration will be rewarded by admiration, celebration and promotion!

Microwave Christians

James 1:3-4: Knowing this, that the trying of your faith worketh patience. But let patience have her perfect work, that ye may be perfect and entire, wanting nothing.

Since the invention of the microwave, Christians have extended that idea to their faith life. They are micro-waving everything including patience! As convenient as that device/appliance is, its usage is still very limited. When you desire a well-prepared delicacy, you need a gas cooker, not a microwave. In the same vein, when you require supernaturally sustainable miracles, you need patience, not a quick-fix prayer!

Acts 12:12 tells of the supersonic speed of prayer and the Bible is rife with thousands of situations where God answered prayers with the speed of light, but yet, the place of patience is cardinal in our Christian life.

Patience is not just a virtue; it is also one of the fruits of the Spirit. Moses wanted to fastforward his destiny (he even killed for God) but God slowed him down and

trained him for forty years! David was very good (killing Goliath wasn't a small feat); yet, God trained him for thirteen years before he became the king of Israel. One year was more than enough time for God to lead the Israelites from Egypt to the Promise Land, but He trained them for forty years! Joseph's dream took about 17 years to happen!

The way Jesus was quoting the Scriptures at the age of twelve, humanly speaking, He could have been ripe for His Ministry earlier than when he was thirty, but God knew better! Nobody can talk of faith today without talking about Abraham (whether the person is a Muslim, a Christian or a Jew), but due to his impatience, Ishmael was born and all the problems in the Arab world can be attributed to that singular mistake! Abraham waited for 25 years during which period about 300 children were born in his household!

You need the gas-cooker much more than you need the micro-wave!

Jesus' Typical Day

It was a great crusade that took place far away from the city with over five thousand people in attendance. Moved by compassion, He preached and healed their sick. Lost in the atmosphere of the miraculous, everybody was oblivious to time. It was almost far into night, and they all needed to trek back to the far away city.

He commanded that they be fed and supernaturally provided food in abundance. Then, He sent away His disciples first before single- handedly bidding farewell to over five thousand men that excluded women and children.

He ought to be exhausted by now, but no. He separated Himself and prayed in the mountain. He updated His father about that day's affair and profusely thanked Him for performing all the miracles through Him.

He was enjoying Himself so much that He lost sense of time. By the time the communion ended, it was already 3:00 am. Essentially, another glorious day has already started.

He started it in a most miraculous way! Walking on water and calming the winds, the waves and the sea!

Brothers and sisters that is a narration of a typical day of Jesus (John 14:13-33) How glorious, how miraculous, how supernatural is your typical day?

Chew Your Cud

Regurgitate is an English verb that means to cause to pour back, especially to cast up (partially digested food). It could also mean to repeat after memorization; "For the exam, you must be able to regurgitate the information".

Animals like goat, sheep, and a few others chew their cuds (the regurgitated food) mostly early in the morning and late at night when there are no foods to feed on.

This process is exactly what the writers of the Joshua 1:8 and Psalm 1:2 had in mind. January is without any doubt, the most reflective month of the year. My prayer is that as you prepare your family budget for the present year; let your meditation be based on God's word. Remember all the wonderful messages you heard in the years gone by and chew them repeatedly morning and night.

Joshua 1:8 - This book of the law shall not depart out of thy mouth; but thou shalt meditate therein day and night, that thou mayest observe to do according to all that is written therein: for then thou shalt make thy way prosperous, and then thou shalt have good success.

Psalm 1:2 - But his delight is in the law of the LORD; and in his law doth he meditate day and night.

I'll Out Run Horses

A land which the LORD thy God careth for: the eyes of the LORD thy God are always upon it, from the beginning of the year even unto the end of the year - Deuteronomy 11:12.

The passing year was glorious
The new year will be victorious
He was, He is, He will be there
He had, He is, He will always care

It may be tough in January
It could be rough in February
Come what may in November
Up to the end of December

He'll be my beginning and end
He'll be my ever present friend
He's the same now & forever
He's in me wherever; forever

This year, I'll collide with forces
This year, I'll outrun horses
This year, I'll be so fruitful
This year, I'll be so yieldful

Numbers Do Not Intimidate God

The difference between a hundred thousand and a million in any currency is an additional zero. The same additional zero separates a hundred million and one billion.

This difference may matter to mortals, but do numbers count with God?

When King Asa needed soldiers to execute a war and realized that he was heavily out-numbered by his enemies, he understood that numbers do not count with God. He prayed one of the sweetest and most touching prayers recorded in the bible...

2 Chronicles 14:11- "And Asa cried unto the LORD his God, and said, LORD, it is nothing with thee to help, whether with many, or with them that have no power: help us, O LORD our God; for we rest on thee, and in thy name we go against this multitude. O LORD, thou art our God; let no man prevail against thee".

Why do you need wealth? To ensure that the gospel of Jesus Christ is preached in China, Indonesia, Malaysia and the entire Middle East? Who should be more concerned about these souls, God or you?

Like King Asa, why not pray to God to add those additional zeros to your finances so that your tithes, offerings, and other giving to your Church may become significant!

You Can Eat Your Cake and Have It!

I read Economics and have a degree in it. Opportunity cost is one of the most important topics we were taught. It simply states that the real cost of any decision is the fore-gone alternative. In other words, if you have $1 million and decided to buy a house instead of a car, the opportunity cost of your house is the car you did not buy.

In one sentence, opportunity cost states that you cannot eat your cake and have it.

The Bible states otherwise. The Bible states that you can eat your cake and have it!

Read 1 Kings 17:14 and Mark 10:29-30.

Whenever you give anything to God, you gain! You do not only have the cake back, you have a multiplied and divinely garnished cake!

The widow of Zarephath gave out a meal but had meals for years! Jesus Christ said that you will have back much more than whatever you give up for God in this world, and Eternal life as well!

Turning Point

Ecclesiastes 11:3 - If the clouds be full of rain, they empty themselves upon the earth: and if the tree fall toward the south, or toward the north, in the place where the tree falleth, there it shall be.

Do you know how to make pap (called ogi or akamu in Nigerian local dialects) or the foreign custard? If you do, you will know that as you keep on pouring the boiled hot water, the pap will (all of a sudden) start turning from watery mixture to a thick paste. Just make sure the water reaches boiling point.

It is the same with prayer. As you keep on pouring your supplications with thanksgiving unto God in the name of Jesus, it's only a matter of time before the answer to your request suddenly turns from spiritual request to physical manifestation. Just make sure your prayer reaches a fervent, heartfelt point.

When the clouds are full of rain, they empty themselves. One remarkable thing is that the weather suddenly turns dark before a very heavy rain. Thus, if things seem to be getting very tough, almost the opposite of what you are praying for, rejoice, your joy is going to be heavy!

1 Kings 18:44 And it came to pass at the seventh time, that he (Elijah's servant) said, Behold, there ariseth a little cloud out of the sea, like a man's hand. And he (Elijah) said, Go up, say unto Ahab, Prepare thy chariot, and get thee down that the rain stop thee not.

Rehab the Prostitute

She sneaked into her room so quietly
Settled into the life she lived so privately
Prostitution, what a life
Old enough to be a wife
To all, she's always ready
The sick and the healthy
The weak and the wealthy
The wretched and the rich

Then that morning…

The knock was faint, so tender
Ten Jewish men? No, they must not enter
What do they want from a mere harlot?
Our fathers did tell us about you
And the mighty works of your Mighty God
About Moses, the Red Sea and all
Our hearts did fail us

Another knock, so loud, so shocking
Jericho Forces? No, they must not enter
What do they want from a lowly outcast?
She hid the Jewish spies
And told her many lies
But, she accepted the God of Israel
Gave up and risked her life for Him

God took note in heaven: Fast-forward…
Jesus Christ is from the lineage of that prostitute
Her name is prominent in Hebrew's hall of faith
Why?
Because "Blessed is he whose transgression is
forgiven, whose sin is covered" (Psalm 32:1)

Rehearsal

Exodus 17:14 And the LORD said unto Moses, Write this for a memorial in a book, and rehearse it in the ears of Joshua: for I will utterly put out the remembrance of Amalek from under heaven.

They all had printed lyrics of the song from where they sang. It was a beautiful worship song which required committed practice. They rehearsed and rehearsed trying to strike an acoustic harmony. Passion was so high; hands were raised to the sky.

The church was packed to overflowing capacity, yet, you could hear a pin drop. The expectation was indescribable. Dressed in spotless crimson, the choir waited to take a cue from the organist.

They started in soft melodious medley that gained momentum with every note. By the time they reached a crescendo, the rapturous ovation could be likened to a volcanic eruption. What a perfect symphony, what a perfect harmony. What a wondrous melody.

Tears of joy flowed freely from every eye of the choir members. All the practice and rehearsals were worth it after all.

Have you been practicing the word of God in your life? Jesus is coming soon. Out of every kindred, and tongue, and people, and nation shall we all sing a perfect symphony to the Lord of Lords and King of kings.
Only those that have been rehearsing will qualify!

Whatever you go through today for the sake of the gospel, count it all joy because your hour of great display is coming!

CNN Advert

Genesis 1:26 - And God said, Let us make man in our image, after our likeness...

There was an advert I watched on CNN which I loved and wonder if you saw it too. Two men were carrying a huge transparent glass in a desert. Outside the glass was a very dry desert with little or no beauty at all. But, when you look through the glass, you will see a beautifully developed scenic landscape, with lush green grass, tall architectural buildings and inviting swimming pools.

That might have been how God created the world from nothing. That same creative power of God has been given to His children such that from the wells of righteousness and from the rivers of living waters within our souls, we can bring forth rivers in the deserts, we can turn Indonesia from being the world's most populous Muslim country to a Christian nation.

We can create super malls from our small shops, produce world-class multinational companies from the four corners of our bedrooms!

Look through the unlimited eyes of God and see that anything and everything is possible!

Psalm 82:6 - I have said, Ye are gods; and all of you are children of the most High.

Eat and Die or Give and Live?

1 Kings 17:12 - And she said, As the LORD thy God liveth, I have not a cake, but an handful of meal in a barrel, and a little oil in a cruse: and, behold, I am gathering two sticks, that I may go in and dress it for me and my son, that we may eat it, and die.

What do you do when God makes a demand on your resources?

Withhold or use them for your personal comfort and perish without hope, or, like the Widow of Zarephath, surrender them to God, partake of it and live a prosperous, fulfilling life today and a glorious endless life with Jesus tomorrow!

The choice is yours, eat and die or give and live!

Is This A World Created By God?

" PULITZER PRIZE " winning photo taken in 1994 during the Sudan famine. The picture depicts a famine stricken child crawling towards an United Nations food camp, located a kilometer away. The vulture is waiting for the child to die so that it can eat it. This picture shocked the whole world. No one knows what happened to the child, including the photographer Kevin Carter who left the place as soon as the photograph was taken. Three months later he committed suicide due to depression.

God created enough resources that will cater for the entire inhabitants of the earth. Unfortunately, only a handful of individuals, organisations and nations have amassed untold wealth to the detriment and (in the above picture, death) of the unfortunate others. What a shame. Jesus' solution for poverty is the gospel! Let's take it to the ends of the earth! It sets men free from all shackles (including poverty) and brings them into their inheritance in Christ!

Kabiyesi

Kabiyesi is a Yoruba (a tribe in Nigeria) word that literally means "who can challenge your authority"? It is used to show the awesomeness of the Yoruba Monarch even when they are obviously wrong. Nobody dares challenge their sovereignty, their powers and their authorities. Their words are laws and their utterances are final.

Now, think about the glory, majesty, splendor and authority of the creator of these mortal kings. He is the King of kings and Lord of lords. We certainly need a stronger word than Kabiyesi to describe Him, yet, the Psalmist calls Him God of faithfulness, without injustice, true and upright is He!

What endears me most to the Almighty God is that in spite of His AWESOME and INFINITE powers; He listens to mere mortals and never abuses His authority. This made the Psalmist ask the very thought-provoking question "what is man that You are mindful of him, and the son of man that You visit him?" (Psalm 8:4).

Yet, Abraham negotiated with this awesome God until He reduced the number of righteous people needed to spare Sodom and Gomorrah from fifty to ten! (Genesis 18:24;32).

Jesus Christ emphatically told the woman whose child was sick that it was not right to give the children's bread (healing) to dogs, but the woman's faith-filled answer made Jesus to change His mind! (Matthew 15:24). God is indeed a gracious, kind, and loving Kabiyesi!

The Queen Mother

I read that the Queen Elisabeth's late mother was a kleptomaniac – she had an irrational urge to steal in the absence of an economic motive. That was truly embarrassing to the world's most celebrated monarch. As a remedy, she was always in the company of aides whose jobs were to instantly pay whoever she 'stole' from. She obviously did not like stealing and tried as much as possible to avoid shops, malls, such places, but, when it was inevitable, provisions were made not to embarrass her.

Born again Christians are like the Queen's mother. They do not like to sin because it is not part of their recreated nature in Christ Jesus, but, if they sin, provision has been made for their sins...

1 John 2:1 - My little children, these things write I unto you, that ye sin not. And if any man sin, we have an advocate with the Father, Jesus Christ the righteous:

Romans 6:1-2 - What shall we say then? Shall we continue in sin, that grace may abound? God forbid. How shall we, that are dead to sin, live any longer therein?

Tom & Jerry

Are you a fan of Tom & Jerry? I am. I've often wondered why this particular cartoon is loved so much by millions of kids around the world. Guess where I found the answer to my question? The Bible!

Do you know that children hardly believe in death? Funny enough, their innocent minds believe in the indestructibility and indomitability of the human spirit. That's why they love Tom & Jerry because those cartoon characters do not die, no matter the kind of weapon they use against each other!

Isaiah 54:17 – No weapon that is formed against thee shall prosper…

The ever-dueling duo (Tom & Jerry) have chased each other from television sets to outer space to cinemas, videos, dvds, etc for over fifty years and have captured the delight and laughter of audience around the world, garnered enough Academy Awards and starred in motion pictures, television and comic books.

Well, I'm sorry if you think I'm trivializing spiritual issues, but, as Christians, are we not supposed to be like Tom & Jerry? Doesn't the Bible say that "We are troubled on every side, yet not distressed; we are perplexed, but not in despair; persecuted, but not forsaken; cast down, but not destroyed (2 Corinthians 4:8-9).

Maybe if we start believing in this God-given fact (much as children love Tom and Jerry), we might just be living a better faith-filled life!

A Tale of Two Women

I once worked in a branch of bank located very close to Sanusi Fafunwa Street in Victoria Island Lagos. I used to come to work by 6:25 in the morning and park my car adjacent to the bank. It was remarkable that an hour later, a lady puts up a small canopy besides the car and begins her business day. She sold telephone recharge cards.

Remarkably, while going home by 9:30 pm, the same spot the card-selling lady vacated by 6:30 pm was occupied by another lady by 9:30 pm and for her night business. She sold her body.

Life is full of choices, but, whatever choice we make, Jesus still loves us in spite of our decisions in life. Maybe what the lady that sold her body needed was somebody to tell her about the love of Jesus.

How many people have you informed about the love of Christ?

At Bethsaida

Thirty and eight years
He still waits in tears
Misty are his eyes
As the angel appears
Nasty are his peers
Blocking his frontiers

As the water is troubled
His excitement is doubled
When will his infirmities end?
When will his realities mend?

Something was different that day
The Master was passing that way
Gazed at Him, did many talk
"Rise, take up thy bed, and walk"
The man was made whole
In spirit, body and soul

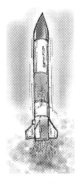

Scud Missile

I don't know who developed or how missiles work. But with my limited understanding, I realized that it must have come from a Bible principle.

God, through a prophet (Micaiah) warned Ahab (King of Israel) and Jehoshaphat (the king of Judah) not to go to war against Syria. Ahab disobeyed God, disguised himself and went to war with the King of Judah. This is the Bible's record of how he died...

1 King 22:34 - And a certain man drew a bow at a venture, and smote the king of Israel between the joints of the harness: wherefore he said unto the driver of his chariot, turn thine hand, and carry me out of the host; for I am wounded.
Scud Missiles when projected hardly miss their targets because they follow the smoke from an enemy plane or some other specific features.

The bow and arrow (missile) that killed King Ahab was guided by the Word of God. The Lord will prepare a table before you in the presence of your enemies, but the unrepentant and stubborn ones will not escape from God's Scud Missiles.

Finally, on a positive note, God's blessings will find you like a Scud Missile – it will not miss its target – you! Remember, Jesus Christ went into the country of the Gadarenes just because of one man, a mad man called Legion. After healing him, Jesus left that country. Do you honestly think you are not as important to Jesus as him? Mark 5:1-20.

Worms

Worms are the numerous relatively small-elongated soft-bodied animals we see around. They are fragile, dirty, and unpleasant. The worst thing about worms is that they are more endangered than most living things easily crushed by their environment, especially by other animals and people.

How would you like to be called a worm?

No matter your situation in life (it doesn't matter if you are less than a worm) God says that He will turn your situation around! Glory be to God!

Isaiah 41:14-15 - Fear not, thou worm Jacob, and ye men of Israel; I will help thee, saith the LORD, and thy redeemer, the Holy One of Israel. Behold, I will make thee a new sharp threshing instrument having teeth: thou shalt thresh the mountains, and beat them small, and shalt make the hills as chaff.

Many years after making this profound statement of fact, God explained to us the reason why:

1 Corinthians 1:27 - But God hath chosen the foolish things of the world to confound the wise; and God hath chosen the weak things of the world to confound the things which are mighty;

Brethren, I'm so glad that I'm a worm of God, because that makes my Maker to take care of me even more.

Eternity

As we walked through the valley of eternity
We danced and mocked, clothed in immortality
O death, where is thy sting
O grave, where is thy victory
Ha ha ha, thou sin, where is thine enticement
Thou impotent fear, why art thou silent

At long last the world embraced love
For ages only symbolized by the dove
The cubs are fed by ewes
Arabs playing with Jews

Like the walls of Jericho they fell
Hatred, prejudice, cultures into hell
Greed, creed, governments, religion
Now united, one people, a holy nation.

Every Second Counts!

Abraham Lincoln was the sixteenth President of the United States (1861-1865). In January 1, 1863, he announced the final Emancipation Proclamation which freed every slave in America. Thus, from that day, every slave was set free under the law of the United States of America to leave his/her slave master/mistress and walk away as a liberated/freed person.

The problem was, not all the slaves heard or knew about this! How sad. Some of them continued being slaves till they died just because of ignorance. A lot of machineries were put in place by concerned former slaves to inform everybody and thanks to their efforts; thousands of slaves were set free because of this.

Jesus Christ has paid the supreme price that sets everybody (from every nation and religion, every tribe and tongue, every race and region, every continent and capital, every land and language) in the world free.

Unfortunately, not everybody is aware of this divine emancipation act of Jesus Christ! That's where you and I come in. Every second counts, every minute matters, millions are dying every second and every minute as slaves to the devil!

The Almighty God, Jesus Christ and the Holy Ghost are counting on you!

Mark 16:15 - And he said unto them, Go ye into all the world, and preach the gospel to every creature.

Matthew 24:14 - And this gospel of the kingdom shall be preached in all the world for a witness unto all nations; and then shall the end come.

The Mirror of Jesus

Proverbs 4:18 - But the path of the just is as the shining light, that shineth more and more unto the perfect day.

Ask any goldsmith and he will tell you that the best way to know if a gold or diamond has been heated to perfection is when you see your own reflection in the precious stone. In the same way, as we look unto Jesus, we progressively change to be like Him:

2 Corinthians 3:18 - But we all, with open face beholding as in a glass the glory of the Lord, are changed into the same image from glory to glory, even as by the Spirit of the Lord.

The heat might be too much for you today – temptations, persecutions, trials, and challenges at work and at home, disappoints and betrayals, etc, but just know that the reason for the too much heat right now in your life is because you are almost perfect! Your life is becoming the perfect reflect of Jesus!

Rare Courage

Hope believes that God can; Faith knows that God will - Author Unknown

The Pharisees told Jesus to hide so that Herod will not kill Him for preaching. This is what He said: Go tell that fox, "I am going to force out demons and heal people today and tomorrow, and three days later I'll be through." (Luke 13:32).

It was decreed that nobody should pray to God. What did Daniel do? Now when Daniel knew that the writing was signed, he went into his house; and his windows being open in his chamber toward Jerusalem, he kneeled upon his knees three times a day, and prayed, and gave thanks before his God, as he did aforetime. (Daniel 6:10).

Paul was told that he would be killed if he went to Jerusalem to preach. This is what he said: "Why are you crying and breaking my heart? I am not only willing to be put in jail for the Lord Jesus. I am even willing to die for him in Jerusalem". (Acts 21:13).

Shadrach, Meshach, and Abednego would not worship any idol even if that would lead to their death. This is what they said: "The God we worship can save us from you and your flaming furnace. But even if he doesn't, we still won't worship your gods and the gold statue you have set up." (Daniel 3:17-18).

Esther risked her life to save the Israelites. Her statement is touching: "Then I will go in to see the king, even if it means I must die." (Esther 4:16).

You Don't Need Motivational Speakers

They are called motivational speakers. Anthony Robbins, Nancy McFadden, Les Brown, Stephen Covey, Napoleon Hill,Deepak Chopra, Denis Waitley, Leo Buscaglia, Jack Canfield, Brian Tracy, Jim Rohn, Harvey Mackay, Zig Ziglar, Wayne Dyer, Phil Mcgraw, John Maxwell, etc. They cover every topic you can imagine.

These people have the power to make people rich, powerful, influential, and successful. How? They don't give people money or any tangible thing you could touch (except course materials). Most times, they don't encourage you to even leave your location. So what exactly give them the power to transform lives? Yes, I found the answer once again in the Bible!

2 Timothy 1:6 - Wherefore I put thee in remembrance that thou stir up the gift of God, which is in thee by the putting on of my hands.

Without a doubt, Paul was the greatest motivational speaker of his time (in fact, every Christian will testify that he could still be considered one of their greatest influences of today). He told Timothy to stir up the gift of God in him!

That's exactly the secret of success! You have all you need to be great, influential, successful, powerful, rich and wealthy. The only thing these motivational speakers do is to awaken the giant inside you, to stir up the gift of God in you!

The good news I want to bring to you today is that if you have the Holy Spirit of God in you, then you do not need any motivational speaker. You can stir up the gift of God in you on your own! There's a victor inside you, there's a blessed man inside of you, there's a champion inside you, there's a giant inside you! Stir it up!

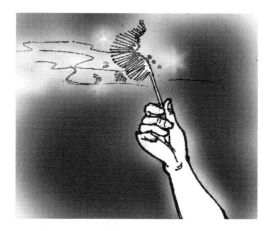

Throw Caution To The Wind

Matthew 26:7 - There came unto him a woman having an alabaster box of very precious ointment, and poured it on his head, as he sat at meat. 8But when his disciples saw it, they had indignation, saying, To what purpose is this waste?

What is your salvation worth to you? Solomon was an illegitimate son of King David. He realized that if not for God, he could not become the King of Israel. He sacrificed recklessly to God (One thousand burnt offerings in just one night. Later he did Ten thousand). He later built God a temple worth $500 billion. That's the much God's love meant to him.

The mad man Jesus casted out legion of demons offered to become a disciple of Jesus. Jesus encouraged him to become an evangelist which he did. He preached in many cities. That was how much God's love meant to him.

A woman anointed Jesus with alabaster box of ointment worth a year and half of a labourer's wage. She indeed lost her mind and threw caution to the wind! That's how much her salvation meant to her.

How much do you love Jesus? How much is your salvation worth to you? How are you expressing this to Him?

What Jesus Never Told Pilate

Pilate saith unto him, What is truth? And when he had said this, he went out again unto the Jews, and saith unto them, I find in him no fault at all. (John 18:38)

Pilate told Jesus that he (Pilate) had the power to release Him (Jesus). He also asked Jesus what truth meant. Jesus realized that Pilate was fulfilling scriptures and didn't respond to him. But, I believe that had Jesus wanted to reply Pilate, He would have said these words and much more:

Dear Pilate, no, you do not have the power to release me. I did not only create you and your parents, I created creation! Without me was anything made that was made, including you Dear Pilate (John 1:3).

Talking about power, Dear Pilate are you aware that all power is given unto me in heaven and in earth (Matthew 28:18) and that you are only fulfilling scriptures?

Dear Pilate, yes, I know what the truth is. I am the truth! Anyone that knows me knows the truth; anybody that has me has the truth. More than that, Infact, I am the way, the truth, and the life: no man cometh unto the Father, but by me (John 14:6). I am also the resurrection and the life (John 11:25) which is why I am permitting you to have your ways.

Dear Pilate I am only laying down my life for a reason, and I have the power to pick it up again (John 10:17). For the joy that is set before me I will endured your ridicule, I will despise the shame (Hebrew 12:2). Because I see my seed that will prolong my days (Isaiah 53:10), I will rather not respond to you Dear Pilate...

Brethren, there is a big lesson for us here: even when we know we are right and are being unjustly treated, because of who we are in Christ, we should just endure the ridicules and despise whatever shame we may face!

Take Away Everything

I just found out that there are only two things that are most important in the life of a believer. Take away everything from a believer and with these two things, he will effortlessly replace them with better ones! With it, you can create and recreate your world, indeed your future! You want to guess?

Let me give you more clues... Job was left with them at a point in his life. Jonah had them in the belly of a whale. Paul and Silas where left with them in a prison. Daniel, Shadrach, Meshach, and Abednego shocked their captors with their demonstration of these two things!

Still guessing? As long as Jesus still held on to these two things on the cross, He couldn't die!

I feel like speaking in tongues...

Brothers and sisters, I'm talking about your faith and your tongue!

Jonah 2:1- Then Jonah prayed unto the LORD his God out of the fish's belly!

Because You Are Sweet

John 15:18 If the world hate you, ye know that it hated me before it hated you.

Have you ever wondered why it happens that any time you drop a cube of sugar, or a drop of honey, or any sweet thing for that matter, just a matter of minutes, ants will come from nowhere to feast on them?

What exactly attracts these ants?

In the game of football, the best coaches always ensure that their best defenders mark their opponent's deadliest scorers! Whenever any attacker has the ball within the eighteen yard box of their opponents, the number of footballers that will try to take him down will be many.

Because you are sweet (how else will I describe you), no matter where you find yourself, you are marked for destruction by satan and his demons. Like a golden fish that has no hiding place, because you are a soul-winner and a kingdom financier, you will always attract giant ants.

But let me also tell you the other things you also attract, it's called goodness and mercy and they shall follow you all the days of your life!

Psalm 23:6 Surely goodness and mercy shall follow me all the days of my life: and I will dwell in the house of the LORD for ever.

Rechargeable Batteries

Isaiah 40:31 But they that wait upon the LORD shall renew their strength; they shall mount up with wings as eagles; they shall run, and not be weary; and they shall walk, and not faint.

I used to use disposal Duracell batteries for all my home appliances (remote controls, clocks, toys, etc) right up to last year. Thereafter, when I got a Sony digital camera, it came with rechargeable batteries. That was when I realize that you can use the same sets of batteries for years. All you need to do is just to charge them whenever you want to use them and their powers are down.

Any believer without the Holy Spirit is akin to a disposable battery. They are easily used up. But if you have the Holy Spirit in you and with you, year after year, month after month, week after week, day after day, hour after hour, minute after minute, second after second, moment after moment, you are ever-ready!!!!!!!!!!!!!

Glorious Oneness

I have always known that we are one with God for in Him we live, move and have our being (Acts 17:28). He calls us the apple of His eyes (Zechariah 2:8), He says that I am graven upon the palms of His hands (Isaiah 49:16), He has said that He will never leave us nor forsake us (Hebrews 13:5), He said that He will be with us always (Matthew 28:20), He never sleeps nor slumbers because of us (Psalms 121:4).

One Sunday, my Pastor brought tears to my eyes with his revelation of our glorious oneness with Jesus Christ!

Remember that Saul (who later became Paul the Apostle) was persecuting the disciples of Jesus. When Jesus had that awesome encounter with Saul, He didn't ask him "why persecutest thou my disciples", this is what Jesus said - And he fell to the earth, and heard a voice saying unto him, Saul, Saul, why persecutest thou me?

Can you see how united we are with Jesus? How closer can it be?

He that eateth my flesh, and drinketh my blood, dwelleth in me, and I in him (John 6:56).

Citation

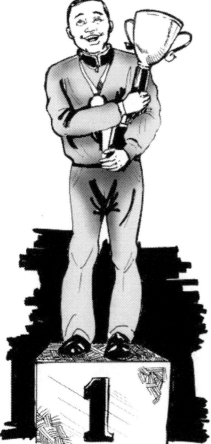

Psalm 87:5-6 - And of Zion it shall be said, This and that man was born in her: and the highest himself shall establish her. The LORD shall count, when he writeth up the people, that this man was born there. Selah

When was the last time you witnessed the citation of a great achiever? Probably at the convocation ceremony of a university or investiture of an institute. You will agree with me that such occasions are always the most memorable in the lives of the recipients.

I am yet to be so honoured. But, I take consolation that my citation is going to be the most memorable anybody could ever desire. Guess why I say so?

Yes you are right, Jesus Christ Himself is not only going to be there, He will shake my hands!!! Brethren, we are all going to witness the most glorious citation ever known to man. Innumerable host of angels, the host of heaven, and a great cloud of witnesses will raptly listen as our exploits here on earth (inspired by the Holy Ghost) shall be read!!!

Time And Chance

Romans 3:26 - To declare, I say, at this time his righteousness: that he might be just, and the justifier of him which believeth in Jesus.

He was born a Levi. He was born a priest. His father was one, so were his grand and great grand fathers. As the high priest of his day, he was in charge of the atonement of the sins of Israel. Unfortunately, he supervised the crucifixion of the same Messiah he had waited for generations for. His name was Caiaphas. After facilitating the atonement of the sins of millions of people, his own sin could not be atoned!

He had been with Jesus for 3 years. He was loved and trusted by Jesus and was His treasurer. He witnessed all His miracles and knew He was the Messiah. Within the last 48 hours of his life, greed took over his senses and after betraying his Master, he could not buy back his life! He killed himself and went to hell. His name was Judas Iscariot.

He was an armed robber. All through his life, he was a thief. He was also violent. He was going to die within the hour. He couldn't care less; he knew he deserved to die. But, wait a minute. Isn't that the Jesus he had heard so much about? The miracle-working Jesus? In spite of what his co-condemned said about Him, this thief called Jesus Lord!

He called Him Lord when He had lost His disciples. When he had been accused, abused, misused, cursed, stricken, mocked, pierced, and ridiculed. Yet, the thief believed in Him and called Him Lord!

Time and chance happened to these three men. Only one (the least qualified) was saved!

Luke 23:42 - And he said unto Jesus, Lord, remember me when thou comest into thy kingdom.

The Weight (Faith) Mechanism

Hebrews 11:29 - By faith they passed through the Red sea as by dry land: which the Egyptians assaying to do were drowned.

Have you ever walked through a door or a gate that operates by the mechanism of weight? Well, if you haven't, this is how it works: There are springs underneath the entrance which are connected to the gates or doors.

The gates or doors open automatically when you are within certain feet or meters in front of them because your weight automatically pushes the springs down and the gate or door opens! Visit Shoprite or the Games at the Palms Mall at Lekki and observe the mighty doors open by your tiny weight!

If you are afraid that the door or gate will not open when you get to it, and therefore stop a few meters or feet away, then, the door or gate will never open!

That is exactly how faith works! The weight of your conviction and confidence in the infallible word of God pushes down adverse circumstances and challenges and opens doors of opportunities and gates of favour whenever a Christian approaches them in faith!

If your faith fails when you are very close to the physical manifestation of your desires, they will never come to pass!

Hebrews 11:30 - By faith the walls of Jericho fell. down, after they were compassed about seven days

God's Children Come Out Richer after Every Economic Recession!

Genesis 26:12 - Then Isaac sowed in that land, and received in the same year an hundredfold: and the LORD blessed him.

In Bible days, there was no fancy name like economic meltdown, global recession, world financial crises; they only had famine, simple.

Anyway, global recession happened in Egypt -by extension the entire world - in the days of Joseph and Pharaoh. Things got so bad that after selling their possessions (including lands), people started selling themselves (enslavement) to Pharaoh! How was it sorted out? God provided the solution through Joseph.

Another economic meltdown happened in days of Elijah. In fact, he was the one that proclaimed it. There was no rain to a point that birds had to feed the prophet! How did it end? God sorted things out through a man of God Elijah. Another recession happened shortly after, the most severe, the most bizarre. Droppings (excreter) from birds were sold for food and people eat their children as food. How did it end? One single prophesy by Elisha ended the economic crisis.

2010. There is economic meltdown, global recession, world financial crises. How will it end? The same God of Isaac, Joseph, Elijah and Elisha is still on the throne. No bail out will work. No economic theory will help. No amount of stimulus package or job creation will sort things out. The Church of Jesus Christ (you and I) are the ones with the solution. The solution lies in adhering strictly to instructions from God!

...And in that same second quarter of 2010, Michael Ogbaa became fruitful, and increased abundantly, and multiplied, and waxed exceeding mighty; and the land was filled with mighty works of faith he wrought through the Holy Ghost (Exodus 1:7 personified).

The Same Pillar, Different Results!

And the angel of God, which went before the camp of Israel, removed and went behind them; and the pillar of the cloud went from before their face, and stood behind them: And it came between the camp of the Egyptians and the camp of Israel; and it was a cloud and darkness to them, but it gave light by night to these: so that the one came not near the other all the night (Exodus 14:19-20).

When the Israelites were leaving Egypt, one of the many miracles God performed was that He used the same pillar of cloud to achieve two directly opposite outcomes through the awesome power of His Holy Ghost. The pillar of cloud gave light to the children of Israel (His people), but caused stark darkness to envelop the entire Egyptian camp!

If it is true that Jesus Christ is the same yesterday and today and forever (Hebrew 13:8), will God not do same thing for His children today? What I'm trying to say is that during this same economic meltdown, global crisis, and great depression, when people are losing jobs, God's children will be promoted! When others are facing mortgage problems, God's children will be buying up houses! When companies (small and big) are going bankrupt, God's children will be establishing and buying up international multinationals! When the entire world is getting confused and perplexed, God's children, through the help of the Extraordinary Strategist (the Holy Ghost) will be exuding wisdom because Christ has been made unto them wisdom!

The same pillar, different results! The same economy, different fortunes! What's the difference? God, through the agency of His Holy Spirit gave His beloved children unfair advantage! Just in case you still require further proof, then read 2 Corinthians 4:6 and discover that God specializes in commanding light out of darkness!

God Doesn't See The Giants, Why Should You?

Numbers 14:8-9 - If the LORD delight in us, then he will bring us into this land, and give it us; a land which floweth with milk and honey. Only rebel not ye against the LORD, neither fear ye the people of the land; for they are bread for us: their defence is departed from them, and the LORD is with us: fear them not.

When God promised the Israelites that He was going to give them a land flowing with milk and honey, He did not inform them that there were going to be giants in those lands, nor that He was going to kill all the giants for them. Why?

Because the giants were inconsequential as far as God is concerned! In God's Sovereign reasoning, those giants should be bread for His children, small objects

with which His children should train their faith with! At the age of 85, Caleb drove away the giants and possessed Hebron (Joshua 14:12).

The same way God gave the Israelites of old, the Promised Land flowing with milk and honey, with the giants in them, His blessings for you this year will come with big difficulties, challenges, obstacles and distractions. Cheer up, they should be bread for you, they should be small objects with which you should exercise and grow your faith!

I can't wait for your testimonies on how you drove away your giants and possessed your possessions!

Roll Call Of Faith Workers

Hebrews 11:6 - But without faith it is impossible to please him: for he that cometh to God must believe that he is, and that he is a rewarder of them that diligently seek him.

If the author and writer of Hebrews 11 was a man, there was no way Samson and Rehab's names would have made the roll call of the hall of faith! If it was authored by a man, he would have devoted the entire chapter to discuss the impatience of Abraham that resulted to his having Ismael before Isaac. He would have discussed Moses' anger, Jacob's scheming, Rehab's harlotry and lies, Gideon's doubts, David's amorous moves and abuse of executive powers, Samson's lusts, etc.

Thanks be unto God for looking only at wonderful act of faith of His children! God does not sit down to count sins (2 Corinthians 5:19), rather, He covers them (Romans 4:7)!

What am trying to pass across to you is that you should remain focused on your bold walk of faith - study, practice and confess God's words. Other distractions are inconsequential to God! When He compiles another roll call of hall of faith with our names boldly written, like He did in Hebrews 11, nothing about our frailties as men will be recorded!

Faith With Deadlines

The reason some of us fail to receive remarkable result in our faith walk is because our believing is often times, open-ended, without deadlines.

David's faith had a deadline when he told Goliath of Gath, "This day will the LORD deliver thee into mine hand; and I will smite thee, and take thine head from thee; and I will give the carcases of the host of the Philistines this day unto the fowls of the air, and to the wild beasts of the earth; that all the earth may know that there is a God in Israel - (1 Samuel 17:46). The host of heaven backed David's faith up immediately and urgently because it has a deadline!

Elisha's faith had a deadline when he prophesied concerning the economy of Israel that "Hear ye the word of the LORD; Thus saith the LORD, To morrow about this time shall a measure of fine flour be sold for a shekel, and two measures of barley for a shekel, in the gate of Samaria – (2 Kings 7:1). Since the scriptures cannot be broken (John 10:35), heaven ensured that Elisha's words never fall to the ground.

Jesus' faith had a deadline when He proclaimed to the hearing of the host of heaven, the earth and everything beneath the earth that "Destroy this temple, and in three days I will raise it up". Jesus resurrected in three days in fulfillment of these words!

More examples abound in the scriptures, but, the point is this... these faith proclamations were made by the power of the Holy Spirit of God through these men of God! The bible says that the same Spirit that raised up Jesus from the dead dwells in you (Romans 8:11)! Go ahead and add a deadline to your faith and see the host of heaven back up your faith-filled words with action! The scriptures cannot be broken!

When The Chips Are Down

Daniel 2:10 - The Chaldeans answered before the king, and said, There is not a man upon the earth that can shew the king's matter: therefore there is no king, lord, nor ruler, that asked such things at any magician, or astrologer, or Chaldean.

Magicians, soothsayers, diviners, astrologers and Chaldeans could interpret dreams, but when the chips were down, only Daniel could do what no man born of a woman could do - tell the king his dream and interpret it!

Pharaoh's magicians repeated all the signs and wonders Moses performed, but, a time came when they could no longer match God and helplessly submitted to His divine purposes!

Read it again, Goliath said the exactly same things David said but, when the chips were down, it was obvious that the one with empty threats lost his life while the one whose claims were backed by God prevailed!

Why am I recounting these stories? I am trying to encourage you to hold on to your faith. Do not give up. Unbelievers may seem to be getting even better results than you, but, it's only a matter of time! The chips will soon be down.

Coal and gold may look alike in their natural states. But test them with fire and you will see the difference!

Fret Not

Genesis 50:20 - But as for you, ye thought evil against me; but God meant it unto good, to bring to pass, as it is this day, to save much people alive.

Our future, to God, is history because as Alpha and Omega, He lives in eternity where He sees the end from the beginning and the beginning from the end! In other words, our aspirations are His recollections.

God knew exactly when famine will engulf the entire Egypt and environs (which included His beloved Israel) and started doing something many years before the event unfolded.

One man was central to God's plan. His name was Joseph. Because of him, Israel was preserved! Only God knows when and how the present - economic meltdown/global economic crises/call it what you like - will end and He has already done something about it even though the world is yet to understand His mechanization.

Good News! You and I are central to God's plans and purposes! How do I know that?

Because I know that all things work together for good to them that love God, to them who are the called according to his purpose (Romans 8:28). Because I have not seen the righteous forsaken, nor his seed begging bread (Psalm 37:25). Because darkness shall cover the earth, and gross darkness the people: but the LORD shall arise upon thee, and his glory shall be seen upon thee (Isaiah 60:2). Because it was at times like this that our great grandfather, Isaac sowed in (an impossible) land, and received in the same year an hundredfold: and the LORD blessed him (Genesis 26:12). Most importantly, because you and I are Abraham's seed and heir according to the promise (Galatians 3:29); joint-heirs with Christ (Romans 8:17).

Can you now understand why I do not join other people to fret or complain about the economic downturn?

Can God Be Surprised?

Hebrews 4:3 - ...although the works were finished from the foundation of the world.

Can anything surprise God?

No. Nothing can surprise God. He lives in eternity. He is the beginning and the end. His works were finished from the foundation of the world! Revelation 1:8 - I am Alpha and Omega, the beginning and the ending, saith the Lord, which is, and which was, and which is to come, the Almighty.

However, when Jesus was here on earth, He marveled twice – because of the lack of faith of the people from His hometown (Mark 6:6), and because of the great faith exhibited by the Roman Centurion (Matthew 8:10).

Jesus has finished His works and is seated at the right hand of God (Hebrew 12:2). But in Acts 7:55, at the sheer faith of Stephen, Jesus had to stand up to acknowledge and received that great anointed son!

Beloved, God cannot be surprised, but, He can be pleasantly surprised when His children exhibit great acts of faith. I have always believed that God must have danced in heaven the day Joshua commanded the sun to stand still! The day David dared Goliath in His name! The day ...

Can you make God do another divine dance with the host of heavenly angels by your acts of faith today!

Who Commanded Light Out Of Darkness

2 Corinthians 4:6 - For God, who commanded the light to shine out of darkness, hath shined in our hearts, to give the light of the knowledge of the glory of God in the face of Jesus Christ.

Only God can command light out of darkness! His raw material for creating light is darkness! In the same way, He commands healing out of sickness, joy out of disappointment, untold riches out of penury, life out of death and beauty out of aches.

In case you need examples – He enthroned Joseph as Egyptian Prime Minister from prison. He turned a chief persecutor to a chief preacher (Paul), and a shepherd boy to a King (David).

Which is easier for God, commanding light to shine out of darkness or turning (fill in you present circumstance) into (fill in your heart desire).

Isaiah 61:3 - To appoint unto them that mourn in Zion, to give unto them beauty for ashes, the oil of joy for mourning, the garment of praise for the spirit of heaviness; that they might be called trees of righteousness, the planting of the LORD, that he might be glorified.

Far Above

Ephesians 2:6 - And hath raised us up together, and made us sit together in heavenly places in Christ Jesus.

Traffic light can stop pedestrians, cars, bicycles and motorcycles here on earth. But, an airplane flying thousands of miles above the earth is unconcerned with the traffic light!

The Bible says that we are seated with Jesus Christ in heavenly places, far above mundane things like sickness, poverty, victimization, and other trivial issues. We are far above these things!

Jesus is seated at the right hand of God -- place of authority! This is where decisions are made! If we are seated together with Jesus, if it's true that as He is, so are we in this world, it only means that there is no decision that can be made concerning by anybody without our knowledge and permission!

Artificial Rain

Ecclesiastes 11:3 - If the clouds be full of rain, they empty themselves upon the earth...

Some regions in China are presently experiencing severe drought. It has become so severe that crops and animals are dying. I watched on CNN how their government, with the help of their military, uses science to send some chemicals into the atmosphere to create "artificial" rain.

I noticed that these man-made rain fell in a funny way – during hot afternoons, sparsely, without lightening or thunder, etc.

Then I remembered the opening verse ... if the clouds be full of rain, they empty themselves upon the earth...
What the Chinese are doing is akin to

cooking egusi soup (a melon soup mostly made by the Igbo and Yoruba tribes in Nigeria) with a microwave oven...

That's also how some Christians treat their confessions and prayers – they are hardly heartfelt, earnest and continued. (James 5:16 – The earnest (heartfelt, continued) prayer of a righteous man makes tremendous power available [dynamic in its working].

Do not misunderstand me, God can answer prayers with the speed of light (remember that the disciples of Jesus were still praying for Peter's release when he showed up), but, true, tested, and sustainable prayers are seasoned with persistence, consistence and sincerity.

Emergency Numbers

2 Chronicles 16:12 - And Asa in the thirty and ninth year of his reign was diseased in his feet, until his disease was exceeding great: yet in his disease he sought not to the LORD, but to the physicians.

Unbelievers have emergency numbers that they call when they run into trouble which are beyond them. These numbers belong to their medical doctors, lawyers, police, bankers, friends and relatives. Unfortunately, most times, in spite of their spirited help, these frantic callers still suffer the calamities of their fate!

I also have emergency numbers. They, however, belong to my spiritual leaders. The beautiful thing about my emergency numbers is that once I am able to reach any of them, no matter the situation, the issues are 100% solved all the time. The situation can be anything - health, legal, security, financial, emotional, relational, occupational, etc.

Why is this so? 2 Chronicles 20:20 says "Believe in the LORD your God, so shall ye be established; believe his prophets, so shall ye prosper". James 5:14 says "Is any sick among you? Let him call for the elders of the church". 1 Corinthians 6:3 says "Know ye not that we shall judge angels? How much more things that pertain to this life? ". Psalm 118:8 says "It is better to trust in the LORD than to put confidence in man."

Do you want to change your emergency numbers?

Spirit Money

Matthew 17:27 - Notwithstanding, lest we should offend them, go thou to the sea, and cast an hook, and take up the fish that first cometh up; and when thou hast opened his mouth, thou shalt find a piece of money: that take, and give unto them for me and thee.

Judas Iscariot was the treasurer of Jesus. It could have been proper for Jesus to have collected money from Judas to pay tax for Himself and for Peter. However, He called forth spirit money.

Spiritual monies are special funding by God for specific and special needs of His ministry. I have always wondered why Jesus sent Peter, but, the Holy Spirit reminded me that Peter became a disciple of Jesus because of miracle. At the words of Jesus, he caught the greatest fish from the most unlikely place! Thus, he became "doubtless" at the words of Jesus!

Are spirit monies still possible today? You might as well ask, can God still fund His special and specific needs through any of His children that have witnessed financial miracles and miraculous financing?

Like Peter, can you be "stupid" enough to go looking for money in the mouth of a fish? In other words, can you trust that God can provide you with your special seeds, precious seeds, project giving and special offering through the most bizarre means?

Yes I can!

...Go Tell His Disciples and Peter

What sin have you committed lately that you are almost killing yourself over it? The Spirit of God has asked me to tell you that while God abhors sin, He loves the sinner!

Peter denied Jesus Christ trice before Jesus was crucified. He was very distraught and thought that his own had finished. But the Angel of the Lord that appeared to Mary Magdalene at the tomb of Jesus made this beautiful statement...

Mark 16:7 - But go your way, tell his disciples and Peter that he goeth before you into Galilee: there shall ye see him, as he said unto you.

Question – Was Peter not one of the disciples? Why was his name mentioned specifically?

Answer – Jesus wanted Peter to know that no sin was big enough to separate him from His love!

The same thing applies to you today – no matter the enormity of your sin (even when you are caught in the act of fornication), Jesus wants you to "go, and sin no more" - John 8:11

Defying The Limits

When you believe in the God with Whom all things are possible, you will always achieve the impossible!

Only God and Moses saw the divided Red Sea before the children of Israel walked across it. Caleb, Joshua and Jehovah were the only ones who witnessed the Promised Land before the soles of ordinary men walked the street! For Joshua to pray to God to hold the sun from setting, I believe he knew it was possible (what do you think?).

In the whole Israel, only the Lord and David saw beyond Goliath! Elijah, Elisha and Jehovah were the only ones that believed that God was taking Elijah in a blaze of glory!

Mary was the only one in the whole world that knew that it was possible for God to incubate in the body of a man! Peter was the only one that knew that a man could walk with a God on water!

God is still waiting for anyone that will be daring enough to divide the red sea, hold the sun still, ride the whirlwinds into glory, break down the walls of Jericho with shouts of victory, walk on the water, etc.

Yes, He's waiting for you!

Satan also sows...

Galatians 6:7 - Be not deceived; God is not mocked: for whatsoever a man soweth, that shall he also reap.

Life is a big garden where the unending process of sowing and reaping takes place. We are already aware that what and how we sow determines what and how we reap. However, I just want to remind us that we are not the only ones that are sowing in the gardens of our life. Satan does too...

Matthew 13:25 - but while men slept, his enemy came and sowed tares among the wheat and went his way

A Christian is said to be sleeping when he stops studying God's words, praying, attending Christian meetings, confessing the word of God, etc. When these happen, the devil sneaks in and start planting his evil seeds of doubt, worry, sorrow, pain, sickness, poverty, strive, death, envy, greed, malice, violence, fornication, adultery, adulatory, etc.

What should we do? 2 Timothy 4:2 - Preach the word! Be ready in season and out of season. Convince, rebuke, exhort, with all longsuffering and teaching. Do not leave your garden of life fallow... Jeremiah 4:3 - Break up your fallow ground, and sow not among thorns. Study, meditate and confess the word of God day and night (Joshua 1:8).

When The Flood Ended

Genesis 6:9 - This is the account of Noah. Noah was a righteous man, blameless among the people of his time, and he walked with God.

Have you ever wondered how much it cost Noah to build the ark God instructed him to build? Where and how did he get the resources to fund God's project? How about all the animals (male and female of every kind) he took with him? Did he buy or borrowed them? How about his home and earthly possessions? Did Noah leave them behind just to obey God's instructions?

The bible did not answer all these questions in details, but, the bible makes it clear that there are always unfathomable blessings that come from obeying God's instructions.

When the flood subsided and Noah's ark settled on the new earth, who do you think had the certificate of occupancy to the entire world?

When Jesus used Peter's boat to preach for a few hours, didn't He immediately reward him with fish harvest that Peter never witnessed in his life?

Has God changed? His blessings are always wrapped up in His instructions, always. How do you respond to God's instructions? What do you do with God's instructions? Proverbs 4:13 -Take fast hold of instruction; let her not go: keep her; for she is thy life.

Work It

2 Kings4: 31- Gehazi went on ahead and laid the staff on the boy's face, but there was no sound or response. So Gehazi went back to meet Elisha and told him, "The boy has not awakened."

In the past, have you by your thoughts, utterances or actions displayed, like Gehazi above, that the word of God did not work? I love Elisha. Immediately he received the unspeakable information from his aid-de-camp, he went with him to prove to him without a doubt that God's words are infallible they work 100% at all times!!!

Matthew 17:19 - Then came the disciples to Jesus apart, and said, Why could not we cast him out?

After answering this question from His disciples, Jesus Christ also proved to His disciples that God's words CANNOT NOT WORK!

All you need is faith and the determination that you will not let go until you have what the word says!

Never ever say as a Christian that the word of God does not work! Work it!